Language Lea....g
with Digital Video

Cambridge Handbooks for Language Teachers

This series, now with over 50 titles, offers practical ideas, techniques and activities for the teaching of English and other languages providing inspiration for both teachers and trainers.

Recent titles in this series:

Language Learning with Digital Video

Ben Goldstein and Paul Driver

Consultant and editor: Scott Thornbury

CAMBRIDGE
UNIVERSITY PRESS

CAMBRIDGE
UNIVERSITY PRESS

University Printing House, Cambridge CB2 8BS, United Kingdom

Cambridge University Press is part of the University of Cambridge.

It furthers the University's mission by disseminating knowledge in the pursuit of
education, learning and research at the highest international levels of excellence.

www.cambridge.org
Information on this title: www.cambridge.org/9781107634640

First published 2015

Printed in the United Kingdom by Hobbs the Printers Ltd

A catalogue record for this publication is available from the British Library

ISBN 978-1-107-63464-0 Paperback

Contents

Thanks

The authors would like to thank Scott Thornbury and Karen Momber for their support and belief in the project, as well as all the editorial team at Cambridge University Press (Ros Henderson, Jacqueline French and Miranda Steel) for their hard work.

Ben: I'd also like to thank Dani for all his help and support during the project.

Paul: A special thanks to Ben for inviting me to join him on this adventure, and also to my wife, Célia and my sister, Julie, for all the support and inspiration they provided along the way.

Acknowledgements

The authors and publishers acknowledge the following sources of copyright material and are grateful for the permissions granted. While every effort has been made, it has not always been possible to identify the sources of all the material used, or to trace all copyright holders. If any omissions are brought to our notice, we will be happy to include the appropriate acknowledgements on reprinting.

Text

Al Boardman for the text on p. 69 from the film *The Power of Video* by Al Boardman. Reproduced with permission;
Pedro Serrazina for the text on p. 103 from the film *Estória do Gato e da Lua* by Pedro Serrazina. Reproduced with permission;
Penguin Books Limited and Penguin Group USA for the text on p. 109 from *The Ball Is Round* by David Goldblatt, published by Penguin Books, 2006. Copyright © David Goldblatt 2006. Used by permission of Riverhead Books, an imprint of Penguin Group (USA) LLC and Penguin Books Limited.

Photos

The publishers are grateful to the following for permission to reproduce copyright photographs and material:
p. 26: Rex Features/© Moviestore Collection; p. 53 (all): © Ted Chung; p. 104 (all): © Pedro Serrazina; p. 106: © Andrew Hinton; p. 108: © Sanpathit Tavijaroen; p. 112: © Abbey Kerr; pp. 119, 120, 135, 157, 163, 165, 173: © Paul Driver; p. 188 (TL): Alamy/© Gary Roebuck; p. 188 (TC): © Paul Driver; p. 188 (TR): Shutterstock/© Anton Balazh; p. 194: © Paul Driver.
Cover image © Doug Aitken, sleepwalkers, 2007. Courtesy 303 Gallery, New York; Galerie Eva Presenhuber, Zürich; Victoria Miro Gallery, London; and Regen Projects, Los Angeles and Corbis/© James Leynse (photo).

Video

Thank you to the filmmakers for the videos used on the ELT YouTube Channel (bit.ly/CUPDigitalVideo):
Amar by Andrew Hinton, Pilgrim Films Limited. Reproduced with permission;
Estória do Gato e da Lua by Pedro Serrazina. Reproduced with permission;
Forgetfulness by Andria Minott, Head Gear Animation. From *Questions About Angels* by Billy Collins, copyright © 1991. Reproduced with permission of Head Gear Animation, the University of Pittsburgh Press and Chris Calhoun Agency, copyright © Billy Collins;
It's In Your Hands by Andrew Hinton, Pilgrim Films Limited. Reproduced with permission;
Like a Fever Dream by Marco Aslan. Reproduced with permission;
Little Big World: Sweet Spain by Joerg Daiber, Spoonfilm. Reproduced with permission;
The Man Who Lived On His Bike by Guillaume Blanchet. Reproduced with permission;
The Power of Video by Al Boardman. Reproduced with permission;
A Thousand Words by Ted Chung. Reproduced with permission;
TMB Bank 'Panyee FC' by The Leo Burnett Group, TMB Bank and The Glue Society. Reproduced with permission.

Introduction

1 The moving image

For well over fifty years,[1] language teachers have been using the moving image both in and outside the classroom. Back in the early 1990s, video was seen as a reward, a form of light relief. It was viewed as a leisure-time activity probably because of its association with television and the idea of passive viewing. You typically showed a video on a Friday afternoon after a hard week's grammar. In those days, the video could consist of an hour or more of a popular film. Sometimes this was even shown for its own sake; in other words, there was not necessarily any task designed around it. Learners could give a summary of what had happened or initiate a discussion based on the video's content, but generally speaking, the video was poorly exploited and not integrated into the lesson.

From being very much peripheral to the main business of language learning, the moving image has shifted to becoming a prime source of content. Not only that, but learner-created video is now as central a focus in the classroom as material introduced by the teacher or institution.

Such a shift clearly echoes what is going on in society at large. The moving image is taking centre stage in our everyday landscape of communication: 'What we are now seeing is the gradual ascendance of the moving image as the primary mode of communication around the world: one that transcends languages, cultures and borders.' (Apkon, 2013, p. 24)

Learners can now access video material at home and on the move, via smartphones and tablets. Watching a film on a big screen in the darkness of the cinema surrounded by strangers has been replaced by the possibility of watching the same thing on a shrunken phone-size screen in isolation and just about anywhere with an internet connection. Likewise, what was once encased in a VHS box or a plastic DVD jacket – very much a separate entity – is now fully integrated into our other classroom materials and is made available via video podcast (vodcast), online streaming or as downloads.

Video has been instrumental in changing concepts of classroom space and settings. In a 'flipped' or decentralized classroom scenario, video is the only form of input or instruction, with the learners accessing this information online at home, while the classroom space is given over to discussion, negotiation and the sharing of ideas. Such a paradigm shift radically changes the role of teacher and learner, with the former no longer being seen as the 'sage on the stage' but the 'guide on the side'.

However, in less radical environments, the presence of video is equally evident. In any online distance course taught on a learning management system (LMS) such as Canvas or Moodle, the moving image can play a major part – both learners and teachers can leave video messages to each other, and teachers can record video tutorials as an effective and more personal way to give feedback. Such interaction is possible in any platform which includes the possibility of a forum or discussion board where learners can interact, and a library where personal files (such as video) can be uploaded.

---

[1] The earliest paper we could find on the subject dates back to 1947: J. E. Travis, 'The Use of the Film in Language Teaching and Learning', *ELT Journal*, 1, 6 (1947): 145–9. Available at: eltj.oxfordjournals.org/content/1/6/145.extract

Why use video?

What has not changed in this shift from analogue to digital is the interest language teachers have in the medium *per se*. In a series of interviews undertaken with teachers on the subject of video, the following reasons were frequently given for using video in the language classroom:

'It's dynamic, and it's what our learners are watching outside class.'
'It takes you into another world.'
'It's a window on the world.'
'It encourages intercultural awareness and critical thinking.'
'Visual stimuli is processed faster in the brain than text.'
'Being visually literate is an increasingly necessary skill these days.'
'Authentic videos provide an enormous amount of cultural information economically.'
'We can take in so much more information if it is presented visually or in combination with text.'
'It makes learning more memorable.'
'People connect to visual content, it engages them.'
'Video is a powerful motivational tool for learners.'

Taking up that last point, how much more motivational if the learners produce the videos themselves? Importantly, YouTube and other sites and platforms have blurred the divide between creator and viewer; nowadays we are all users. The plethora of self-made or self-edited videos on such sites show how we can manipulate and select what we want, when we want it (for more on remix culture and mash-ups, see Part 1 Introduction, Section 2: *Genres*, on page 15). For this reason, this book is divided into two main parts: *Video exploitation* and *Video creation*.

Likewise, people make and share videos to tell stories about their lives, remixing home videos with elements from popular culture (football, music, etc.), thus creating new genres. Video remix has also become a highly influential genre in the political arena: the 'Yes We Can' parodies were good examples in the United States, while in Spain 'the relaxing *café con leche*' viral video series was borne out of a speech made by the Mayoress of Madrid (see youtu.be/cRObfG3I-Q4). As Chris Ware says, 'We could say that the primary gesture of the film spectator in the digital era is to impose oneself onto the film, redirecting its flow and in time, perhaps, re-editing its content.' (2009, pp. 140–1)

You will see that many of the tasks in this book focus on this remix culture and the possibilities this opens up for learners and teachers.

Purposes

Much has been spoken about the techniques for using the moving image. There have been countless books and websites referring to activity types, exploitation techniques and different genres[2], but little, however, has been said about the role of moving images in itself, nor about the pedagogical advantages of using video, say over audio or written text.

[2] For example, titles such as Ulrike Meinhof's *Language Learning in the Age of Satellite Television* and Jane Sherman's *Using Authentic Video in the Language Classroom* were published in the late 1990s and early 2000s.

We have to go back to video's early days to find an in-depth discussion of its pedagogical role. At the time when video emerged in a major way in the language classroom, Jane Willis published a paper (1983) in which she established certain key roles for video in the classroom.

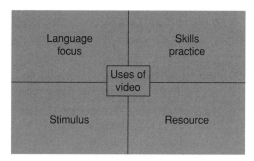

Figure 0.1: Key roles for video in the classroom (adapted from Willis, 1983)

Firstly, there is *Language focus*. As its name suggests, the main idea behind this is that the video sequence presents a language model: new or recently introduced language items such as grammar structures, words or chunks are encountered in context. Here, the video medium is treated a little like audio with little attention to the visual stimuli. However, a sequence could be exploited without sound to give visual clues in order to elicit and practise specific language items.

The second role of video is *Skills practice*, that is, the use of video to practise the skills of listening and (to a lesser extent) reading, and as a model for speaking and (to a lesser extent) writing. Within this group, there is the classic use of video for listening comprehension, based on both language items and the overall structure of the text. This involves practising micro-skills such as listening for specific information or gist and speculating about visual content, as well as prediction and hypothesizing. With regards to speaking, the class would view particular target situations which learners could then re-enact in simple role plays, as a complement to functional language / speaking sections in textbooks (e.g. giving directions). The target language is made available in a wider variety of situations and in increasingly longer sequences, perhaps in naturalistic contexts (e.g. discourse markers in everyday speech). Reading and writing tasks that provide skills practice might include the reading and reproduction of subtitles, intertitles or other textual elements in a video.

The third role is as *Stimulus*. Here the moving image acts as a way to engage interest and is a catalyst for follow-up classroom tasks such as summarizing (e.g. retelling a narrative) or discussions not necessarily based on the intended message of the video. In this case, the video can be 'silent' as comprehension-based activities are not required: the learners could be engaged with the visual content only. Alternatively, the video could be part of a longer task sequence, involving first comprehension and then some kind of active response. The moving image as stimulus provides the learners with a far more interactive role and logically leads to the creation of their own work, such as the writing and recording of a dialogue or a soundtrack.

Finally, the fourth role is as a *Resource* in which the video is a source of information and provides learners with the content for subsequent tasks such as project work. There is clearly a connection with CLIL (Content and Language Integrated Learning) here, in which learners gain knowledge about the world through English. An extension of this function would be the use of video to provide direct instruction, such as in the case of the 'flipped classroom'.

Each of the activities in the book will include two of these four main roles (one as a primary learning focus and one as a secondary learning focus) in the activity outline so you can be sure of their overall aim. However, in Part 2: *Video creation* the learning focus may also be technical, related to the filming, editing and remixing of the videos themselves.

2 Moving images in the digital age

In recent years there has been an increased awareness of the need for focused teaching activities based on video or moving images. The term *video*, of course, no longer refers to reels of videotape, but has been co-opted to mean any moving image that is filmed and broadcast using digital means. Owing to the impact of this digital media in our work and daily lives, we are now more accustomed to accessing information and producing our own input via the moving image. At the time of writing, statistics from Cisco Systems indicate that video will soon account for 62% of all consumer internet traffic.

Computers, tablets and smartphones now incorporate video cameras, making it possible to film an event anytime and anywhere. This is blurring the distinction between the amateur and professional, the formal and informal, and the verbal and visual.

Sites such as YouTube and Vimeo facilitate the online sharing and creation of such video material. Because of these advances, people are accessing these videos and producing their own at an increasingly early age, making video material that can compete with the professionals or critique mainstream sources. Such videos are accessed by hyperlinks and can be embedded into a blog, a tweet, etc. allowing people to customize and personalize the material to an even greater extent. It is revealing, after all, that the strapline for YouTube is 'Broadcast Yourself'.

For example, it is commonplace for 'YouTubers' to upload their own version of the highlights of a football match, editing the action, creating their own captions and then placing their own soundtrack over the top. It is interesting to see how elements of popular culture – football, avatars and rap music – merge in these multi-modal creations (that is to say, media that incorporate a variety of modes, such as a text, images and hyperlinks). In the same way, the YouTube generation often create their own spoof versions of well-known videos such as adverts. On occasions, these versions can 'go viral' and become so popular that they can, ironically, enter the mainstream (for example, a rap version of a McDonald's commercial was 'adopted' and became an official advert for the company). Thus, we could say that digital media has freed up and democratized 'the visual', giving more people the chance to communicate visually than ever before. Through Creative Commons licences (one of several copyright licences that allows the distribution of copyrighted works), the greater accessibility and availability of original video material is guaranteed.

Likewise, social networking sites such as Facebook and Twitter have helped new communities, often associated with artefacts from popular culture, to emerge. Video clearly plays an important role in such communities. For example, participants in a particular video game[3] may create a forum in

---

[3] Another term which now has a far broader reach than previously because of the number of new devices and platforms that are used to play them, such as personal computers, consoles and smartphones. Video games have become an art form as well as an industry.

which to discuss their interests (very often using English as a lingua franca). James Gee and Elizabeth Hayes (2011, pp. 69ff.) call these forums 'passionate affinity spaces' because the participants share a particular interest which they feel strongly about. They suggest that these spaces provide new learning systems which are very different in nature from traditional classrooms. In addition, new programs or tools are constantly appearing to facilitate the presentation, accessibility, editing and delivery of this video material.

Bearing in mind all the above, it may well be that video is becoming the preferred medium for entertainment and information presentation and the chief cultural resource for many young people, and this is, of course, having a growing impact on teaching environments as well. Such developments offer huge potential for teachers wanting to work with moving images. For example, there's a good chance that learners' motivation will increase if they are given the opportunity to work with video in both a critical and a creative way.

3 Moving images and language

Gee and Hayes argue that digital media (which clearly includes video) is a powerful force precisely because it can 'power up' language, granting it new abilities (2011, p. 9). Images (moving or still) reinforce text and vice versa, and for learners this is an undeniably rich context, granting them greater opportunities and more diverse ways to communicate.

Consider a voice chat program such as Skype which allows us to speak to others across the globe in real time, either one-to-one or in groups, without being physically present. Likewise, asynchronous tools allow us to create video profiles. Learners write questions and the video persona you have created answers them. The tool provides a record of the question-and-answer exchanges that the learners can carry out – convenient if teachers wish to highlight a specific exchange for either content or language purposes. Such interactions are *embodied* and *situated* (Gee and Hayes's terms) in a landscape that is entirely new.

Indeed, many people now spend more time engaging in this kind of communication than talking to their neighbours face-to-face. The challenge open to language teachers is how best to exploit these new spaces for communication and interaction with learners.

Multi-modality, narrative and 'deep media'

Multi-modal texts are now more pervasive than ever before. Compare reading an online newspaper today with one from 50 years ago – the experience has changed beyond all recognition, with scrolling and touch screens altering the way in which we engage with word and image. Even the most academic of texts may now juxtapose words, still and moving images, while the written word itself can also become 'animated' with presentation software such as Prezi, techniques like kinetic typography or through 'word cloud' software such as Wordle (wordle.net).

To 'unpack' such texts requires new skills, and the speed at which you can identify, filter and categorize information and the ability to decode and encode visual images form part of what is known as *digital literacy*.

However, the Internet does not serve only as a way of re-transmitting familiar formats, as a new delivery mechanism for old media. As Frank Rose has said, a new multi-modal narrative form is emerging: 'The Internet is the first medium that can act like all media – it can be text, or audio, or video, or all of the above. It is non-linear … it is inherently participatory and often game-like, and that's designed above all to be immersive. This is deep media.' (2011, p. 3)

Andy Goodwyn goes on to say: 'It [the Internet] has become the most multi-modal medium and the one where consumption and production are the most authentically interrelated.' (2004, p. 119).

Of course, there are recurring skills and literacies that come into play when participating with this media. As Gunther Kress (2003, pp. 173–4) put it (as far back as 2003) on watching his son and friends multi-task at their Playstations:

> All the games make use of the visual, but they make use of much more: there is a musical score, there is rudimentary dialogue, and there is writing usually in a box above the rest of the visually saturated screen. There are an astonishing range of skills and abilities at issue here …

The implications for the language classroom are that we need to tap into these new narratives and literacies as well as taking advantage of the enormous learning possibilities that the 'digital surround' offers us. This means encouraging learners' 'critical participation as cultural producers in their own right', as Buckingham (cited in Goodwyn, 2004) put it in the context of media education. Such an approach is equally valid in the language classroom, and the activities that you will find in this handbook are an attempt to do so, going beyond purely linguistic aims at times.

4 How to use this book

Although we have opted to divide the 'exploitation' and 'creation' ideas in this book, this is more to facilitate navigation. Books are, after all, bound by their limitations as physical media. It is not our intention to imply that there is, in any way, some kind of exploitation/creation dualism. Often the activities in one part may flow seamlessly into the other through, for example:

Thematic links, such as *Views about news* (3.5, Exploitation) and *Campaign* (6.6, Creation), which both draw attention to the art of public speaking.

Learning focus, such as *Reconstruct the plot* (2.4, Exploitation) and *Tube talk* (8.7, Creation), which centre on use of the narrative tenses.

Procedure, such as *Mini Bollywood* (2.3, Exploitation) and *Body swap* (7.7, Creation), which both require the synchronization of a narrative with moving images.

Video genre, such as *Ads A: techniques* (3.1, Exploitation) and *Trope* (9.3, Creation), which both examine the persuasive techniques used in advertising.

Similarly, we draw no hard lines between activities that take place inside or outside the classroom. Digital tools and technologies have made the once hermetically sealed walls of the classroom quite permeable. If the goal is to empower learners to use English as a tool at work or in their everyday lives, then we should provide opportunities for them to practise in as many different contexts as possible. While some activities are still well-suited for the classroom, others extend online to take advantage of collaboration tools and the time afforded for critical thinking by asynchronous communication. Mobile devices are brought into play as hubs for creative media production as well as content consumption, not only within the classroom but also at home. Several projects push these devices to their (current) limits, not only calling upon their abilities to record and edit multiple video and audio tracks, but also deploying the functionality of location awareness and digital cartography to tie and situate language in the hustle and bustle of busy towns and urban centres. At the same time, we bring the outside world into the classroom through videos that will broaden perspectives and take learners on journeys of the imagination.

We also draw no lines between different types of media, as learners will be encouraged to mercilessly dismantle, deconstruct, detach, split, rebuild, create and mash up audio, video, text, images and games. For all of these reasons, we recommend that the reader take a similar approach to using this book. Take a playful stance and feel free to ignore the lines that divide categories, technologies, tools and procedures. Remix and mash up activities as you see fit. Have fun.

5 Practical advice

At the end of the book, you'll find a list of useful links to websites and sources for video. There is an extended version on the book's online product page (www.cambridge.org/9781107634640), which will be updated to take into account new sites and the disappearance of old ones. Please also visit the authors' companion website for this book: digitalv.net. You will also find practical tips related to hardware and software in the introduction to Part 2: *Video creation*, pp. 119–125.

Finally, when using video from any online source, it is advisable that you watch the clip first to check for anything taboo. You should also be aware that offensive comments may sometimes appear below the clips. It's always a good idea to check for this before giving learners a task, even if you are not intending to focus on the comments themselves. You can avoid this altogether by downloading or embedding the clip in a class web page or blog so the comments wouldn't be visible to learners, or by using a tool which removes all peripheral texts such as adverts and comments (for example, quietube. com). However, please check the permissions associated with any clip before doing any of these things (see 'Copyright issues', p. 17).

References

Apkon, S. (2013) *The Age of the Image: Redefining Literacy in a World of Screens*, New York: Farrar, Straus & Giroux.

Gee, J. P. and Hayes, E. R. (2011) *Language and Learning in the Digital Age*, New York: Routledge.

Goodwyn, A. (2004) *English Teaching and the Moving Image*, London: Routledge Falmer.

Kress, G. (2003) *Literacy in the New Media Age*, New York: Routledge.

Meinhof, U. H. (1998) *Language Learning in the Age of Satellite Television*, Oxford: Oxford University Press.

Rose, F. (2011) *The Art of Immersion*, New York: Norton.

Sherman, J. (2003) *Using Authentic Video in the Language Classroom*, Cambridge: Cambridge University Press.

Ware, C. (2009) 'Viewer participation', in Nicholas Rombes (ed.) *Cinema in the Digital Age*, pp. 140–141, London: Wallflower Press.

Willis, J. (1983) 'Implications for the exploitation of video in the EFL classroom', in J. McGovern (ed.) *Video Applications in English Language Teaching, ELT Documents*: 114, pp. 29–42, London: Pergamon Press.

Part 1:   Video exploitation

Introduction

1 Activity types

A brief history

It is interesting to see that video-based activities have, over the last decades, moved from very controlled, language-based tasks to comprehension-based ones and then to exploring a much freer role. *Language focus* tasks were adopted by early video English courses such as the BBC's *Follow Me* (from 1979). However, they are still used today on a whole host of online English language courses. For example, some of Vicki Hollett's *Simple English Videos* (www.simpleenglishvideos.com) focus on language items that are particularly problematic for language learners. The items are embedded in short dialogues that are used to exemplify the difference between them (for example, between *interesting* and *interested* or *sympathetic* and *nice*).

Early video courses such as *Follow Me* included these short sequences or exchanges to highlight specific language items. However, within the same episode, they would also offer longer sequences in the form of comedy sketches. This was something taken up by a number of ELT ready-made video products such as *Grapevine* (Oxford University Press, early 1990s) which adopted elements of roles 1 and 2 (see Introduction, pp. 3–4 for a closer analysis of the key roles of video in the classroom) within a situation comedy or mini-drama storyline using professional comic actors. The chosen genre emphasized once again the light-hearted quality that it seemed video material was required to possess. Here, the target language was intended to be comprehensible and repeated by the learners with the emphasis on *Skills practice* – listening comprehension and after-you-watch speaking.

In the 1990s, the concept of 'active viewing' was established. Here the learner took a more active role than that of the passive viewer and the teacher began to use the interface more: freeze-framing with the remote control, segmenting long videos into shorter scenes, removing and adding subtitles, playing a video without sound, covering the screen and so on. Learners were also divided up into groups for information gap tasks such as jigsaw viewing. Although there were logistical difficulties with these kinds of activities, many of them are still pedagogically valid today.

More recently, shorter clips chosen from sites such as Vimeo or YouTube have become popular source material for educators, especially those with little or no dialogue so the class is not 'distracted' by comprehension. The tasks are often open-ended and encourage critical thinking, allowing the learners to respond to the content with their own interpretation. Clearly, working with video as *Stimulus* allows learners to focus on narration as well as on more subjective questions such as analysing mood and atmosphere. Using the video as a stimulus also implies that the material itself is seen as the springboard for other activities such as discussion and debate.

Finally, examples of video as a *Resource* can be commonly found on YouTube and other sites. Online English language courses are one example as are TED talks (www.ted.com), Big Think seminars and other instructional sites such as the RSA's animated lectures (www.thersa.org/events/rsaanimate). Language courses are increasingly using video in this role, for example in blended learning programmes where video input informs and enhances the face-to-face classroom.

Sequencing of tasks
The classroom use of film clips, video and other moving image material has generally been sequenced in terms of pre-viewing, while-viewing and post-viewing tasks, although the relative emphasis on each stage and the kinds of tasks involved has varied considerably.

Before you watch
Activities typically set for this stage include prediction tasks based on stills of the video in question or questions posed by the teacher focusing on the learners' own experience or prior knowledge. Other warmer questions typically focus on activating schemata about the topic or genre of the clip to be viewed. For example, if you were going to do an activity on the ever-popular subject of movie trailers (see Activity 3.6: *The art of the trailer*), you might want to brainstorm with learners what makes a successful trailer and what its generic characteristics are. You could also ask if there are any movies that the class would currently like to see based on viewing a trailer. Assuming your learners have seen lots of trailers, you could dig deeper and ask in what way a trailer could spoil your enjoyment of a film (perhaps by showing too much of the action). All of this should activate interest without distracting the learners from the main task at hand.

In one technique that Jamie Keddie calls 'Videotelling'[1], the prediction stage is extended so as to form the body of the lesson, with the actual viewing being the culmination, even reward, for the collaborative questioning, hypothesizing or storytelling that goes on between learners and teacher. However long the 'Before you watch' stage is, eliciting a response from learners and encouraging interest in the clip prior to viewing is clearly the aim. Some other ideas for doing this, including specific prediction tasks, are as follows:

- *Narrate the content or action of the video*
  This helps learners' own visualizations. The more detailed your narration, the more vivid their visualizations. Once learners have visualized the scenes, they should be motivated to compare these with the 'real thing'.

- *Provide plenty of background information and context*
  You could use a review or another related text to engage interest. Be careful of spoilers, though. At the very least, you could refer to or explain any particular place names or cultural references.

- *Preview part of the video in class* (perhaps an easily comprehensible or impactful sequence)
  From this one stand-alone part learners can conjure up a picture of what may come before and after it.

[1] Keddie, J. (2014) *Bringing Online Video Into the Classroom*, Oxford: Oxford University Press. Page 112.

- *Preview some of the key words and expressions in a word cloud*
  Learners can piece together a speech or a particularly important piece of dialogue or simply the
  main topics from a review, a summary or a written description of the movie clip (see Activity 2.1:
  See it, read it, watch it).

While you watch

Such tasks have varied enormously since video became an integral part of a language lesson. In
early video courses, most tasks treated the video in the same way as audio, setting comprehension
questions of the multiple-choice or true/false variety. With the advent of longer videos, it was
customary to divide this watching into various sequences to make the material more accessible, or
to ask learners to watch the same sequence on various occasions, asking different questions each
time.

   If there is a clear language aim, then classic 'while you watch' tasks would be gap-fills in which
target items from the transcript are missing or need to be reordered. Other common tasks carried out
while you watch include ticking items on a list (e.g. objects or people in the video), sequencing items
on a list, taking notes, answering questions (e.g. multiple choice), etc.

   However, the problem with such tasks is that it is asking the learner to do two things at once: focus
on the questions and view the sequence. Also, by focusing only on language, the visual aspect of the
clip is lost. In the digital age, such a problem can be partly alleviated by platforms (such as educanon.
com) which allow the learners to view the video and answer the questions all on one screen.

   The motivation for viewing should be more than simply 'watch and check'. It should be
remembered that the visual message of any moving image sequence provides another whole layer
of meaning. The visual often works alongside the verbal, reinforcing the overall message, but at
times one mode can interfere with another, as when an overly intrusive soundtrack disrupts your
comprehension of the screenplay or your enjoyment of the visual. The following list of alternatives to
the 'while you watch' tasks focuses then on different stimuli – visual, aural, textual and cinematic.

   It is important to point out that the majority of the following tasks are set by the teacher *in advance*
so that learners are viewing and gathering data *while* they watch, but they are more often than not
carried out *after* watching the video. All of the task types below will be included and expanded upon
in separate chapters of the book.

Focus on images/objects

- Narrate what can be seen: images or objects. (This can be easily turned into a memory game for
  younger learners, i.e. *How many people were there?*, *What objects can you see and in what order?*,
  What were they wearing?, etc.)
- Ask learners to recall the colour, size or shape of certain objects and images.

Focus on cinematic elements

- Identify editing techniques: number of shots/cuts/scenes along a timeline (e.g. in a chase scene).
- Identify setting/atmosphere/mood created by lighting, shadows, etc.
- Identify camera movements (handheld, aerial, etc.) and shot types (close-ups, long, point-of-view,
  tracking, etc.) and how these affect our viewing.
- Identify visual clues to classify genre (e.g. special effects, stunts, costumes, etc.).

Focus on cultural aspects
- Identify these aspects in landscape, food, setting, behaviour, social etiquette, etc.
- Encourage critical thinking by identifying stereotypical, idealized, non-representative or anachronistic images.

Focus on text
- Use translation, dictogloss, voiceovers, etc.
- Spot differences between script and on-screen subtitles.
- Read script and predict the way it will be filmed through discussion or a storyboarding task.
- Compare the original spoken narrative with a written summary.
- Write reviews or summaries of video action or compare a simplified version of the script with the authentic one.

Focus on inference
- Identify what characters might be thinking during a sequence based on body language, etc.
- Identify the subtext of a particular scene (e.g. what the characters really mean or feel rather than what they actually say).

Focus on character types
- Identify how body language/clothes/expressions/gestures/emotions point to typical stock characters or types (e.g. hero, villain, sidekick, etc.).
- Idenfity how some stars are associated with particular roles (e.g. Woody Allen).

Focus on sound
- Predict and visualize action from sound only.
- Analyse music, sound effects, different voices, background noises and how they enhance a sense of realism (e.g. creaky floorboards in thrillers, bells chiming, etc.).
- Identify the type of sound (both diegetic: coming from the world of the story or non-diegetic: e.g. voiceover, musical score).
- Identify the link between song lyrics and visual images.
- Compare a radio version of a sequence (e.g. an adaptation) with the original film.

Focus on genre
- Identify the genre of a video from characters, music, atmosphere, etc.
- Identify to what extent a video conforms to a generic formula and where it subverts the genre (e.g. in experimental or viral advertising).
- Identify recurring symbols that carry generic meaning from film to film (e.g. the tin star badge worn by a sheriff in a western).

Focus on narrative
- Identify the temporal relationship between events. Is the narrative chronological or subversive? (e.g. the backwards narrative in the film *Memento*). Are there flashbacks or flashforwards?

- Identify the narrative drive (e.g. the conflict and resolution in a story) and narrative codes (e.g. a flickering light in a sci-fi movie meaning the arrival of extra-terrestrials).
- Say what's happening and predict what's going to happen next.
- Mute the sound and learners guess what is being said or narrated. They can do their own version dubbed over the top.

After you watch

Such tasks are typically summaries or reconstructed narratives. Some of the above 'while you watch' tasks can be reconfigured so that they also appear *after* the viewing process, focusing on the class's memory of events. Learners could complete information-gap activities here if they have been divided into different groups.

These could be closed-answer questions, such as true / false, or open-ended ones. Focusing on purely visual stimuli, learners can, for example, reorder images into a correct sequence or recall the most memorable ones. Elements of the script can be referred to, for example matching characters with particular phrases or correcting parts of a script. Such tasks are valid, but many focus on remembering and comprehending and not higher-order thinking skills such as creation or analysis. For example, if working with an advert, the 'while you watch' task may be simply take notes but the 'after you watch' one could be related to analysing the techniques employed, the market and the message (analysis) and then asking the learners to invent their own (creation). When setting a task, it is therefore important to bear in mind *when* you want the learners to carry them out. As a general rule, it is a good idea to establish the purpose of the tasks prior to watching but not overload the learners while they are watching.

2 Genres

When authentic video started to be used in the language classroom, it was mostly limited to film clips, film adaptations of novels and plays, news bulletins, and some TV programmes such as sitcoms and documentaries. With the arrival of YouTube and video sharing, we can, of course, choose from a far wider selection of genres. There are a number of new and reinvented genres. For example, with regard to advertising, fake, spoof and viral adverts now compete with regular commercials on these video channels and it is sometimes hard to tell the difference between them. Likewise, YouTube has spawned many other new genres like React (youtube.com/playlist?list=PL23C220A2C5ECoFDE) videos, which commonly show two screens – the video content itself and an image of a person reacting to it live. The viewer thus multi-tasks watching both screens at the same time.

Cinema

Traditionally, full-length films were studied in their entirety in class, often accompanied by the literary text to discuss differences between the original and the adaptation. In a flipped classroom scenario, this is still possible but to make better use of classroom time, it is advisable to show shorter clips from films and study these in greater depth. You could focus on these particular topics as sub-sections of the cinema genre: openings and endings, encounters, chase sequences, trailers, voice-overs, telephone conversations, flashbacks, soundtracks, etc. A number of tasks in the book focus on these areas.

Advertising

Adverts are an excellent resource to use in class partly because of their brevity and because they often pack a lot of creative ideas into a short space of time (see Chapter 3: *Video and persuasion*). Furthermore, learners have undoubtedly seen so many adverts in their lives that they will be able to analyse them without too much difficulty and compare them with how these products might be advertised in their own cultures. They can also bring their own adverts in to class.

Areas that can be studied here include the following: use of metaphor and imagery, association of ideas, stereotyping, the use of catchphrases, slogans and other advertising language, types of storytelling used in advertising, humour, etc. New genres such as infomercials and viral marketing campaigns can also be studied.

Advertising is an excellent way to introduce critical-thinking tasks into the classroom as learners question assumptions about certain products and how these are marketed through different techniques which persuade the potential client to consume them.

Critical-thinking tasks can be particularly well applied to charity adverts or campaign clips available online. These are good to exploit in class for a number of reasons: they can provide a strong link with issues you may be working on in class and they show how different cultures treat similar themes such as drink-driving. Learners can evaluate the effectiveness of the campaigns and visualize their own. We can analyse different strategies campaigners use to attract their audience and market an idea or concept, as well as a product.

Music videos

If there is one genre that has successfully reinvented itself in the digital age, it is the music video. Of course, we used to watch such promotional videos on music television (MTV was launched in 1981) while now YouTube and social network sites are the preferred media for viewing music. We share our favourite music videos with our friends in the same way that we might a share the image of a sunset or our pet dog.

Clearly, one of the mosts interesting things about these videos is the relationship between the visuals and the lyrics, so many of the tasks in this book focus on the degree to which the visuals intepret or symbolize the lyrics or simply represent them literally. Another advance is the way the genre has developed in style. Over the years, many well-known film directors have turned the music video into a genre of artistic merit and not the mere capture of a performance.

Finally, digital media has meant that an increasing number of cover versions of well-known songs are suddenly available for online viewing: an example of a global phenomenon that can be personalized and localized to have a particular impact in certain cultures. Nowadays, it does not surprise us to see the sailors of HMS *Ocean* singing 'All I Want for Christmas' (youtu.be/ SDZcGz4vmJc), a Russian police choir performing Daft Punk's 'Get Lucky' (youtu.be/Po8B_lBULoE) or a thousand teenagers doing amateur versions from the comfort of their own bedrooms. Sometimes, these amateur fan videos get more hits than a performer's official version.

Television programmes

Arguably more of us now watch video online or on mobile devices than on television sets. We also watch more amateur videos than professional these days, but conventional television programmes can still be exploited to great effect in the classroom. Select from genres such as sitcoms, game shows, drama, comedy programmes and reality shows, as well these ideas for non-fiction clips: highlights of sports events (useful for learners to practise their own commentaries), interviews (again interesting to get students to role play after viewing), programme trailers, documentaries (wildlife programmes are excellent for analysing different types of shots), cookery programmes (great to compare written and spoken discourse) and speeches (great for body language and emphatic language). Other options include different kinds of news such as bulletins, current affairs reports, eye-witness or 'fly-on-the-wall' reports; makeover and lifestyle shows; travel programmes; 'how-to' and science videos. Again, many of these genres are covered in tasks in the book.

Mash-ups, remixes and the YouTube generation

The fact that the YouTube generation can now play around with other people's content and invent their own visual mash-ups or collages is both highly creative and empowering. In the same way that rap can subvert musical traditions by mixing unlikely elements together to create a unique sound, the same is true of video makers working with hybrid forms. The process of making meaning through connection with other texts and media is known as *intertextuality*. Intertextuality forms the basis of many humorous programmes, for example when serious genres such as documentaries are ironized or subverted in *docu-soaps* or the words of one person are made to come out of the mouth of another.

Mash-ups are particularly prevalent in the world of music videos. When a cult song comes along like the Korean 'Gangnam Style' (in its day the most viewed video on YouTube), it spawns a number of different mash-ups. A famous example was that created by mashing-up 'Gangnam Style' with music and action from the movie *Ghostbusters* so that two songs are seamlessly linked both visually and aurally.

A different example is the mash-up of Lionel Richie's song 'Hello' created by Matthijs Vlot (see Activity 4.5: *Mash-up madness*). It consists of 43 very short clips crammed into about 80 seconds. The clips come from a number of Hollywood films so that the words said by the actors in the clips sync with the lyrics. There are many websites, such as MashVault (mashvault.com) where you can access clips of this type. However, tech tools are becoming so sophisticated that the mash-up genre is liable to evolve still further. For example, a recent video for Bob Dylan's classic 'Like a Rolling Stone' (video.bobdylan.com/desktop.html) is interactive, allowing viewers to zap through 16 television channels as a variety of television personalities lip-sync the lyrics. The stations you can sample include a cooking show, a tennis match, a children's cartoon, BBC News and a live video of Dylan playing 'Like a Rolling Stone' in 1966: as such, it's a perfect example of intertextuality.

Videos like this are undeniably fun to use in class but, like many other short-but-sweet movies available on YouTube and other sites, the original content is often brief and ephemeral and sometimes only engages lower-order cognitive skills like remembering and describing. While high on entertainment value, the visual jokes and pranks so common to YouTube do not provide much scope for exploitation. This brings us on to the whole issue of how to choose video material.

3 Criteria for selection

With a plethora of video content at hand, it is easy to get saturated by it all. At the same time, it can be very time-consuming and distracting to find the 'right' video sequence online. For this reason, the majority of the activities here represent generic frameworks which you can interpret for your own context and the resources which are available to you. There are guidelines in each activity for alternative video sequences that can be exploited, but there will surely be others that would suit your particular context or the time in which you choose to show the video. Hopefully, these generic activities will provide inspiration for you to go and seek out those videos.

There are, however, some general guidelines that you should bear in mind when selecting a video.

- *The role of the video and the issue of comprehension*
  If its purpose is language focus, then comprehension of spoken language will be all important. Bear in mind that authentic material may be overly demanding. If showing a documentary, for example, consider grading the voice-over so learners pick up on particular structures or lexical items more easily. The visual material remains the same so learners may not feel patronised.

    If the role of the video is a stimulus (for example, to stimulate interest in another task), the need to comprehend language may not be an issue at all. In such cases, you could use the same video with many different levels, precisely because comprehension is not a key concern. It then becomes a question of grading the task not the input.

- *The length and pace of the video*
  Choose short sequences, where possible, especially if there is a focus on language or skills practice. In common with the great majority of videos on YouTube or those posted in social media, very few of the clips suggested in this book are over five minutes long. If, however, you are interested in learners responding to visual stimuli alone, the video can be a little longer. If the learners view the video first at home, then time restrictions do not apply in the same way.

- *The interface*
  Bear in mind that some websites provide subtitles and the entire transcript of a video (e.g. trackable transcripts in TED talks) – this can save you a lot of preparation time and eases the cognitive load on the learner considerably. Likewise, consider the digital tools that you have available in class and that the students have at home. Avoid setting tasks which some learners will be unable to do because of any technical restrictions.

- *Viewing in or outside class*
  If choosing a clip to be viewed outside class, you could access sites which are ideal for self-study (e.g. English Central: www.englishcentral.com) or longer clips with a high information load.

    If choosing a clip for in-class use, make sure the clip has sufficient potential to generate a number of different tasks and that these tasks generate language. A common error is to put on a video; the learners are entertained but remain passive viewers. Consider the different angles that you could adopt when learners view the video: cultural, cinematic, narrative (see above for 'while you watch' task types).

- *Relevance / interest value*
  The video clip you choose should, where possible, be relevant to the learners' lives and experience and relate in some way to the topics and / or language that you are focusing on in class. Try to integrate the video activities with other tasks that learners can do outside the classroom (e.g. making their own version of a video that you show in class) so that the link with the learners' world is apparent to them.

- *Allow learners their say*
  Be flexible enough to allow learners to introduce their own videos in class, either made or selected by them. Get them to record a video log so that they don't lose track of the clips. However, check beforehand for any inappropriate language or content. Indeed, make sure you do this for all material that you select for class.

4 Copyright issues

As Stephen Apkon[1] has commented, the intense popularity of YouTube and other video-sharing sites has meant we are now 'part of a global visual conversation' (2013, p. 23), blurring the distinction between creators and consumers. The mainstream will continue to provide content but amateurs can now make something just as interesting and share it just as quickly. In order to critique a video, users very often interact with each other's content, creating parodies and mash-ups. This raises important questions of copyright: When can we edit or 'borrow' other people's content and for what purposes?

Uploading videos to a video-sharing site

YouTube include copious information on their site about copyright, warning users not to upload content which has not been made by themselves or which they are not authorized to use (youtube. com/yt/copyright). As you would expect, you can also watch a video about this, available at the same link. Other video-sharing sites will contain similar information (for example, vimeo.com/help/faq/legal-stuff/copyright).

Using YouTube (or similar) videos online

When a person uploads a video on to YouTube, Vimeo or any other sharing site, they can specify whether their video can be embedded on to another website. You should take care to check the specifications and permissions associated with any clip before attempting to embed it onto a separate website for teaching purposes.

Downloading YouTube videos for classroom and other uses

There are many tools and applications that allow you to 'grab' online videos from sites such as YouTube[2]. However, doing this is a breach of copyright. We advise that you do not download YouTube clips in this way.

General advice

It is inevitable that you will see examples of online videos that have violated copyright. Indeed, a lot of material you will find on video-sharing sites is of this nature. This, unfortunately, does not justify you

---

[1] Apkon, S. (2013) *The Age of the Image: Redefining Literacy in a World of Screens*, New York: Farrar, Straus & Giroux.
[2] These include ClipGrab and YTD Video Downloader.

doing the same. If in doubt about whether it is legal to show a clip in class, ask your learners to watch the video in question at home and base an activity around it to do subsequently in class.

Disclaimer: *The information provided in this Copyright section is correct to the authors' knowledge at the time of publication. This section is no way intended to be taken as legal advice. It is the opinion of the authors.*

1 Video and text

This chapter looks at the role of voice-overs, subtitles, captions, scripts, screenplays and thought bubbles – in other words, the *text* that accompanies a video sequence. The popularity of today's 'silent movies' (videos that include no written or spoken word at all) on YouTube and Vimeo has meant that many teachers have forgotten or overlooked the importance of exploiting text and image. It is easy to get seduced by the beauty of these silent clips, many of which are emotionally charged and supported by moving soundtracks. However, the techniques by which these short and silent clips are exploited tend to be repetitive, for example, memorization or description of the visual stimuli. They often don't engage higher-order thinking skills.

For me, it is precisely its multi-modal quality that makes the moving image such a rich medium. One of the most positive contributions that the moving image has made in recent times is the way that it can enhance and bring to life a text of some complexity. In this respect, visual poems and visual adaptations of lectures can help these texts reach a wider and a more diverse audience.[1] (See Activity 1.7: *Dialogues* for ideas on how to exploit these kinds of multi-modal texts and Activity 5.5: *Memory* as an example of a visual poem.)

Working with the text alongside the moving image is nothing new in language teaching. A technique that was first popularized by the advent of the communicative approach was the information gap, in which the class was divided: for example, half the class watched the screen (without sound) while others read the script or subtitles. However, apart from being logistically complicated to arrange in class, I found that such tasks didn't motivate learners a great deal. There clearly was an information gap to be completed and this generated a fair amount of language; however, learners didn't have to create a text themselves to do the activity but simply summarize or reformulate what had been said by others.

What the following tasks have in common is that the learners are creating their *own* texts, categorizations or visualizations. This should motivate them to then check against the original version and notice any differences or similarities between their version and the 'real thing'. In fact, 'noticing' is a common thread running through a number of the tasks in this chapter.

Finally, an interesting aspect of working with multi-modal texts is that at times the different media – text, audio, soundtrack, video or still image – do not necessarily sit happily with each other as they are 'made up of potentially conflicting verbal, visual, and musical codes, where the different codes may be in a contradictory relationship to each other' (Meinhof, 1998, p. 5). Precisely because of these contradictions, the video genre can be an extremely innovative one, with new hybrids being created all the time (for example, see Activity 1.9: *Video-enhanced texts* for another take on a visual poem). This is easily achieved in the digital age as so many people have access to so much material simultaneously. Thus, as adaptations to existing genres are repeated and disseminated, new hybrids emerge. Copying and pasting one text into another can engender surprisingly new meanings.

---

[1] Good examples of this are the visual adaptations of Ken Robinson's lectures produced for the Royal Society of Arts, such as this one on Changing Education Paradigms: (youtu.be/zDZFcDGpL4U).

The text does not always necessarily refer to that found *within* the clip itself but can be one associated with it. See Activity 1.6: *Comment on the comments*, for example, for an analysis of the written comments made about different clips in online sharing sites such as YouTube. These texts play, after all, an important part in how we experience these videos online and may influence our opinion about them.

Finally, consider how text and moving image can be compared in other contexts – for example, a written recipe and how this changes when it is presented orally on film, a 'how-to' video and the written equivalent, a short story and its visual representation, etc. In each case, learners will see how the video enhances the text (see Activity 1.9: *Video-enhanced texts*) though they may also spoil certain visualizations – the images that we conjure up in our imaginations, which are sometimes the most vivid of all.

References

Meinhof, U. H. (1998) *Language Learning in the Age of Satellite Television*, Oxford: Oxford University Press.

1.1 Translate it back

Outline	Learners translate subtitles from their own language to English and then compare with the original to notice differences and similarities.
Primary focus	Language focus: whatever emerges from your selected clip; language of difference and similarity
Secondary focus	Skills practice: writing subtitles
Time	15–30 minutes, depending on length of clip
Level	Intermediate and above
Preparation	Find a video clip (1–2 minutes long) with English dialogue in two versions: (1) with original English subtitles, (2) with learners' L1 subtitles. DVDs include subtitles in a number of languages, so accessing these different versions should be straightforward. Be aware there could be noticeable differences between the L1 and English subtitles. For example, a joke might not be translated literally, or a long piece of speech might be summarized so it fits on the screen, etc.

Procedure

1 Play your selected clip with the sound off but subtitles in the learners' L1 visible. This will give the class a clear idea of the clip's English language content.
2 Learners watch the clip again, translating the subtitles into English. Pause where necessary to allow the learners time to do this.
3 Learners compare translations in pairs or small groups.
4 Play the clip with the sound on and English subtitles visible.
5 Learners identify any differences between their translation and the original dialogue, and discuss these in groups. Here are some possible problem areas to raise with learners:

   - Untranslatable words, expressions or idioms
   - Mistranslations or oversimplifications
   - Differences in register (e.g. the learners' L1 version may be overly formal)
   - Cultural norms causing errors (e.g. transposing proper names)
   - Humour may be untranslatable
   - Long pieces of speech may be paraphrased or summarized. Which parts are missed out? Why? Is the main idea still well expressed?
   - Intonation, tone of voice, gesture (and other aspects of delivery which can't be expressed in written form) may not have been considered

Follow-up

Learners could record their translated versions and dub them over the top of the original clip, thus making their translation 'come alive'. However, there is no need for them to synchronize their speech with that on screen.

Variation 1
The procedure can be reversed with learners seeing the English subtitles first and then the L1 subtitles.

Variation 2
A similar task can be done with dubbed films although this does not allow for such close examination of the dialogue itself.

Variation 3
Learners can watch a sequence from a film in their L1 and translate the subtitles into English. They then compare their subtitles with those produced professionally.

1.2 Change the genre

Outline	Learners change the genre or style of a video clip by writing a new script for it.
Primary focus	Skills practice: writing and narrating a new voice-over
Secondary focus	Stimulus: creating a different genre or style from purely visual stimuli
Time	30–60 minutes
Level	Upper intermediate and above
Preparation	Find a video clip (1–5 minutes long) from any genre. The video should lend itself to being repurposed in a different genre. The *Like a Fever Dream* clip in the example below could be repurposed as an advert, music video or even a documentary. The clip is available on the Cambridge University Press ELT YouTube channel (bit.ly/CUPDigitalVideo). Many 'silent' video clips would also work fine because they are often abstract in nature.

Procedure

1   Play your selected video clip with the sound off. In groups, learners watch and discuss ideas for a new genre for the clip. They also start preparing a short accompanying voice-over. *Important:* the idea is not to recreate the original voice-over but to come up with a new one to go with the learners' selected genre.

2   Play the clip again without sound, freeze-framing where necessary. You may need to repeat the clip several times. Help with any descriptive language and provide guidance with regard to learners' chosen genres. If the groups are writing an advert, they may need assistance with promotional language, such as the use of imperatives, positive adjectives, etc.

3   Play the clip without sound one more time. Learners practise their voice-overs in their groups. Monitor and help with intonation. The differences in genre should also be apparent in the way that the voice-over is read.

4   Finally, play the clip while learners in groups take it in turns to perform their voice-over, synchronizing the script with the on-screen images. If there is no dialogue but some kind of soundtrack (music, noises, etc.), then play this now. Learners discuss how the soundtrack contributes to the atmosphere.

5   Conduct a discussion about the different genres and voice-overs. Learners justify their choice of genre. Other questions to pose:

Which voice-over script did the class like best?
Which matched the images in the most interesting or original way?
What problems did they find with the exercise?

Example

Like a Fever Dream

Link: bit.ly/CUPDigitalVideo

Possible genre
Describing a memory

Possible voice-over script
I remember those roads very well. Driving fast on scenic roads. And I remember the wind on my face, cycling towards the beach. I can see my family, my kids, my nephews and nieces lying on the sand. It's like a black and white photo, although the sunset is in colour. I remember those days when I'm travelling by plane or by bus. The image of that beach and my family, the kids laughing by the pool and me walking towards them with my hands outstretched …

Follow-up
Write an objective description of the action in the video so that learners can see the difference between 'straight' narration and the poetic description above.

1.3 Imagine the scene

Outline	Learners imagine a video sequence from a voice-over or monologue.
Primary focus	Stimulus: using video as a springboard for visualization, in the form of a storyboard
Secondary focus	Language focus: present progressive to narrate activities; language of hypothesis
Time	30–60 minutes
Level	Intermediate and above
Preparation	Find a video clip (1–5 minutes long), from a film, advert or other genre, which contains a voice-over or monologue. You will also need a transcript of the monologue/voice-over. *Important*: the transcript should provide clues to the context and visual aspects of the clip. For example, it could include names of people/places, descriptive language, etc.

Procedure

1 Distribute the transcript of your selected clip and ask learners to read it. Clear up any confusion with regard to unknown lexical items or structures.

2 Ask learners the following questions:

Is the speaker male or female?
How old is the speaker?
How do you know?
What video genre does the monologue/voice-over belong to?
What is the main theme of the monologue/voice-over?

3 Ask learners to brainstorm some visual images that could accompany the transcript. They should justify their choices and provide evidence for them.

4 Learners read the transcript again in pairs or small groups. They visualize an image for different parts of the transcript, creating a mental storyboard to complement the script. Encourage learners to think of the types of shots they want to include – close-up, long shot, aerial view – and other details such as landscape, weather, etc. They should also indicate where there could be a particular shift or change in the kinds of images presented. Allow time for learners to take notes or draw a storyboard.

5 Learners compare their storyboards. Are there differences or similarities between different groups' images?

6 Play the clip and ask learners to compare their ideas with the definitive version. They should identify any differences and similarities.

Note

Good genres for this are documentaries or campaign adverts which carry strong messages and hard-hitting images. The opening sequences of films can also be a good option as these are often dramatic in order to attract the audience's attention. They are also good at setting the scene or establishing themes. However, make sure that you select material in which the text is as compelling an element as the images.

Variation 1

Instead of showing the transcript, use the subtitles and the soundtrack, but cover the rest of the screen. The learners will benefit from listening to sound effects (e.g. police sirens) when attempting to visualize the scene.

Variation 2

The activity could work equally well with dialogue rather than a monologue. However, the questions in Step 2 would need to be adapted accordingly.

Example

Sunset Boulevard

Link for transcript: www.imsdb.com/scripts/Sunset-Blvd.html
(the voice-over runs from: *'Yes, this is Sunset Boulevard ...'* to *'... All I know is they didn't sell.'*)

Images that could be visualised

sunrise	police cars	journalists	cameras
film star	mansion	man in pool	

Images that appear in the clip

name of the street	long avenue with palm trees	long line of cars

Figure 1.1: Still from *Sunset Boulevard*

1.4 Interior monologues

Outline	Learners write their own thought bubbles for a video sequence.
Primary focus	Skills practice: writing thought bubbles; performing in sync with the images
Secondary focus	Stimulus: writing humorous exchanges from visual stimuli, e.g. body language, etc.
Time	30 minutes
Level	Intermediate and above
Preparation	Find a video clip (1–5 minutes long) in which a number of people are present and in which clear reactions are visible (e.g. gestures, facial expressions). The reactions should lend themselves to the writing of thought bubbles. For example, the clip could contain a tense or climactic moment, or one in which a difficult decision is made. Possible sources include dialogues from films and short news items in which something dramatic or unexpected occurs. Speech and thought bubbles can be added to clips using video editors such as Windows Movie Maker, Apple iMovie or similar.

Procedure

1 Play your selected video clip and ask learners to note down any key words that occur to them. For example, they could write down adjectives which describe the characters' behaviour or attitude in the clip.
2 In groups, learners decide which genre the video belongs to (e.g. an advert, a piece of news, a film clip). Their task is then to write the thoughts of the people in the scene.
3 Allow plenty of time for the learners to watch the video several times in class and write out their thought bubbles in complete sentences.
4 Monitor and select a group to read out their thought bubbles in class. Allow the group to rehearse their narration in sequence with the images in the clip.
5 The selected group read out their thoughts as the clip is played.
6 Other groups compare and discuss similarities and differences between their thought bubbles.

Note
To encourage learners to be funny, emphasize that very often we don't say what we are thinking. You could, for instance, choose a scene in which people are behaving very politely but having very impolite thoughts.

Variation 1
If you have an interactive whiteboard (IWB), learners can write their thought bubbles directly onto a paused image on the screen. If learners have access to tablets in class, they may be able to write the thought bubbles without the teacher being at the centre of the task.

Variation 2
Watch the highlights of a football match or any competitive sporting event. Many learners will be familiar with this genre and the kind of commentary that accompanies this action. Learners can consider the difference between the commentator's words and the thoughts that the fans may be having at the same time.

1.5 Intertitles

Outline	Learners write their own intertitles for a video sequence.
Primary focus	Skills practice: summarizing or interrupting a scene with a written description of action or atmosphere
Secondary focus	Language focus: exclamations and dramatic language
Time	30 minutes
Level	Intermediate and above
Preparation	Find a short video clip which contains various noticeable changes in scene, action or atmosphere. For example, your clip could contain scenes before, during and after an important incident.

Procedure

1 Establish with learners what an intertitle is and what it's for (see 'Note' below). Explain that intertitles can describe, summarize or comment on the action. They can also represent the thoughts or words of the characters, or simply link one scene and the next. If you wish, show an example of a clip from a film that has intertitles.

2 Play your selected clip with the sound off. Explain that the learners are going to create intertitles for the clip.

3 In pairs or small groups, learners watch the clip several times and select four or five locations where they would like to insert intertitles. They also write the intertitles themselves.

4 In larger groups, learners compare the position and wording of their intertitles. Did they freeze the action in the same places? Was the wording of the intertitles similar? They decide on the best ones.

5 Play the clip again to the whole class, freeze-framing when told to by selected learners, who then narrate their intertitles live to the rest of the class. Ask them to justify their choice of intertitles.

Note

Intertitles originated during the silent film era (1900s–1930s). They were used to convey dialogue between characters, narrate a scene or add background information not visible in the film itself. A very well-known example is the one-word intertitle 'Suddenly …' from Eisenstein's *Battleship Potemkin*, which introduced a battle immediately after a scene of celebration. In modern cinema, intertitles are often used at the end of a film, for example to describe the epilogue to a story, or what happened to the characters in real life, etc. They are still used as an artistic device in modern cinema and recently were revived in the contemporary silent film *The Artist* (2012).

Figure 1.2: Intertitles

Variation 1

1 Find a clip from a silent film with six to eight original intertitles. Extract the intertitles from the clip using editing software like Windows Movie Maker or Apple iMovie. Alternatively, use an online editor like youtube.com/editor (online editors can be quite basic but they are fine for shorter clips and simple editing). If you don't have the software, simply take screenshots of the intertitles or write them out yourself.
2 Establish the theme of the film and its characters where necessary.
3 Project the intertitles to learners in a mixed-up order, or distribute them on a handout. Learners guess the correct order.
4 Show learners the clip so they can check the order of the intertitles.

Variation 2

Select a video clip which contains many background noises. Learners write subtitles for hard-of-hearing people, for example: door creaks, footsteps, dog barks, wind blows, alarm goes off, etc.

1.6 Comment on the comments

Outline	Learners read and analyse the comments made on YouTube or other online media that feature video.
Primary focus	Skills practice: writing comments; categorizing and interpreting comments
Secondary focus	Language focus: giving opinions and interpreting comments
Time	30–60 minutes
Level	Pre-intermediate and above
Preparation	Find a video clip that has generated some controversy or divided opinion in online media. Getty Images' *From Love to Bingo* (youtu.be/E7xc7J8bdsU) is used in the example below. Another suitable clip is Frans Hofmeester's time-lapse videos of his children, *Evolution* (youtube.com/user/Hofmeester?feature=watch).

Procedure

1 Briefly explain the background to your selected clip. There is no need to conduct an extended analysis of the clip itself, since the focus here in this activity is equally on the clip and the viewers' comments.

2 Play the clip and get learners' initial reactions. What do they think of the technique, the story, the overall effect?

3 Ask learners to anticipate the types of reactions viewers might have to the clip. They should think of both positive and negative reactions.

4 Show learners a selection of comments about the clip from YouTube or other online media. Ask them to categorize these into positive, negative or neutral. Were they similar to the reactions they had anticipated?

5 Learners discuss which comments they agree or disagree with. Are any of the comments inaccurate or too extreme? This would be a good moment to pick out key opinion adjectives to reinforce this lexical area.

6 Learners note down their own comments about the clip and read them out. Is there a consensus in class or are there radically differing opinions?

7 For the next class, ask learners to bring a video clip of their choice to class, together with a variety of comments.

Example

From Love to Bingo

Link: youtu.be/E7xc7J8bdsU

Background
The clip consists of 873 images shown at 15 images per second, giving the impression that you are watching a film rather than a series of unrelated still images.

Possible positive reactions
Technically impressive, originality, length of time it took to research/produce

Possible negative reactions
Speed of images is overwhelming, the individual images are bland

Viewers' comments
A really old idea
Brilliant … and a true story for many of us
It really scared me :(
Amazing to have the vision and patience to create this
Story is great but images themselves are dull
A work of art! Every time I watch it I see something new
Gave me a headache!

Note
Comments can be found on YouTube or Vimeo but also in news media articles about these videos. Despite the best efforts of YouTube and Vimeo to filter offensive remarks, many such comments can still be found online. Please be aware of this when setting the task for your class.

Variation
The task can be useful for teaching the language of opinions more explicitly. Learners can find and make a record of expressions they like in the comments, and use them themselves to comment on other video clips.

1.7 Dialogues

Outline	Learners read and analyse a dialogue taken from a video clip.
Primary focus	Stimulus: identifying elements within a dialogue; predicting
Secondary focus	Skills practice: role playing a dialogue
Time	45–60 minutes
Level	Pre-intermediate and above
Preparation	Find a video clip in which the dialogue itself acts as an engaging standalone text that will stimulate learners' imaginations. It is a good idea to use a context which could then be role played by learners, perhaps a typical transactional dialogue but with a twist. Interviews are a good option because they lend themselves well to the subsequent role play. You could choose everyday interviews or highly dramatic ones, for example between police and suspects in crime series such as CSI. Famous interviews from films would also work, such as the memorable encounter between Jodie Foster and Anthony Hopkins in *The Silence of the Lambs*, in which Foster explains the significance of the film's title. Prepare transcripts of the clip's dialogue, making sure that each new speaker's turn starts on a separate line.

Procedure

1 Distribute the dialogue transcript from your selected clip to the class. Ask learners to consider all or some of these questions, depending on the nature of the dialogue:

Who is speaking? How many people are speaking?
What are they talking about?
Where are the speakers?
In what context could they be speaking?
What makes it different from a conventional dialogue?
Are there any expressions you understand but that you wouldn't use yourself?
What evidence do you have for the above answers?

2 Once you have dealt with any doubts about vocabulary, ask the learners to act out the dialogue in pairs or small groups. At this stage, ask them to use whatever stress and intonation patterns they think are appropriate to try to make the dialogue 'come to life'.

3 Play the video clip to the whole class, freeze-framing where appropriate. Present learners with the following questions:

What differences are there between your performance of the dialogue and the real thing?
What clues in the transcript did you interpret rightly or wrongly?
What surprised you about the characters, the context and the tone of the conversation?

4 Learners act out the dialogue again, taking on board their responses to the questions in Stage 3.

1.8 Video dictogloss

Outline	Learners watch a video and then reconstruct its dialogue from memory.
Primary focus	Skills practice: identifying elements within a dialogue; prediction; role playing dialogue; listening for specific language items
Secondary focus	Resource: recreating dialogue to replicate the original script
Time	30–60 minutes
Level	Intermediate and above
Preparation	Find a video clip in which the dialogue itself acts as an engaging and accessible standalone text. The dialogue must be clear and between 30 and 60 seconds in length. You can select a dialogue to illustrate a particular language item or structure.

Procedure

1 Play your selected clip with the sound off. Working in groups, learners guess the topic of the conversation by looking at body language, gestures etc.
2 Learners watch the video again with the sound on. They try to understand as much as possible, individually taking brief notes. Remind them to write down only key words or very short phrases, not whole sentences. Repeat this step as many times as necessary, allowing learners to expand their notes each time they listen.
3 Learners work in pairs and compare their notes. Each pair then tries to build their notes into a complete dialogue, making it as similar to the original as possible.
4 Learners then work in larger groups, comparing their reconstructed dialogues and negotiating any further improvements or changes.
5 Play the clip again with the sound on. The different groups compare their consensus version with the original and notice any differences.
6 Learners role play their version of the dialogue.

Note

The dictogloss is an effective way to help learners focus on detailed features of language that they may not otherwise notice. The traditional dictogloss with audio is a classic variant on dictation. However, in this case the visual cues help learners considerably in reconstructing the dialogue. Once learners have been through the transcript, you could show subtitles and ask the class to identify any differences between the actual spoken language and the captions.

Variation

Divide the class into two groups, A and B. Group A concentrates on taking notes based on one character's side of the dialogue, and Group B focuses on the other character. After Step 2, pair up learners from Group A with learners from Group B so that they piece together the two halves of the dialogue. Allow them to make up parts that they didn't understand or can't remember. Learners can then perform their versions before comparing with the original.

1.9 Video-enhanced texts

Outline	Learners read a poem or a song, visualize it and then watch a video version of it.
Primary focus	Resource: visualizing and describing mental images; deciding how video can enhance a song or poem
Secondary focus	Stimulus: note-taking; memorization; finding connections between image and text
Time	30–60 minutes
Level	Pre-intermediate and above (examples here for pre-intermediate)
Preparation	Find a video clip of a poem or song that is accessible in terms of level and is related to a current class topic (the example below is about the theme of love). You will also need a transcript of the poem or song. Ideally, choose a video clip which is not a straight performance. If possible, the action should reflect the words of the poem or song in a more indirect way. A good source for videos of poems is Moving Poems (movingpoems.com).

Procedure

1   Learners listen to your selected poem or song being read aloud. You can do this live or make a recording beforehand. Ask learners the following questions:

Do they recognize it?
What genre does it belong to?
What is the main emotion/theme of the poem/song?

2   Distribute the transcript of the poem or song. Depending on its length or difficulty, you could jumble up the text so that the learners have to order it from memory. Check the answers with the class.

3   Ask learners to visualize images which might appear in the accompanying video. What clues in the lyrics helped them come to this visualization? If your learners like drawing, get them to sketch some of their ideas. If the poem or song was used for an advert or other specific purpose, ask the learners to imagine what that could be.

4   Play the video clip and get learners' initial responses to it. Are the images close to what they had visualized? Does the visual accompaniment go well with the poem or song, or not?

5   Play the clip again, allowing learners to take notes on the visual aspects of the clip. What elements can they remember? How do these elements connect with the words/lyrics? Is there a direct connection (what you see is what you hear) or is it more indirect/abstract?

6   Finish with these discussion questions:

Would you say that the moving images enhance the song/poem?
Do they add another level to it? If so, in what way?
Do you think video clips help people appreciate poetry and song, or is it best to just read or listen?

Follow-up
Learners find their own visual poems or songs and bring them to the class in the next lesson.

Example

[i carry your heart with me (i carry it in] **by E. E. Cummings**

Link for poem: poetryfoundation.org/poem/179622

On Vimeo alone, there about twenty different visual interpretations of this poem.
Ask the class to view a selection of these visual interpretations and to analyse their differences and similarities. For example:

How many of them include the text itself?
Is the poem read in its entirety? If so, who by?
What difference does this make?
Who features in the video, what are they doing?
What visual elements from the poem are included?

Note

There are a number of visual poems that use kinetic typography, or animated text, allowing learners to see as well as hear the words of the poem. See also Activity 5.5: *Memory* for an activity based around the visual poem *Forgetfulness*.

1.10 **The art of the title**

Outline	Learners watch a series of title sequences, analyse them and then try to create their own.
Primary focus	Resource: discussing different title sequences and identifying genres
Secondary focus	Language focus: vocabulary of cinematic genres
Time	30–60 minutes
Level	Intermediate and above
Preparation	Find three or four video clips with memorable or inspiring title sequences. Good choices are films directed by Alfred Hitchcock or Pedro Almodóvar, as well as James Bond films, where illustration and kinetic typography (animated text) create a particular 'look'. It's also advisable to choose films from different genres, styles and eras, and to include some sequences that learners will recognize. Sequences can come from films in any language, not just English. To save you time, you could show this collage of famous title sequences: bit.ly/LcTPpI

Procedure

1 Learners reflect on title sequences of films. Present them with the following questions:

How long are typical title sequences? Why are they important?
Do title sequences always precede the action or vice versa? Why?
Do they only include credits for the actors, film producers, etc.? What other information might you find?
How does the soundtrack contribute to the atmosphere created in the title sequence? (For example, James Bond films often include memorable songs which form part of the film's identity.)
How does the graphic design and typography influence how we read the information in the title sequences?

2 Play your selected title sequences. Pause during each one to allow learners to identify any films that they recognize. In pairs, they should also discuss the possible genre of the film and guess when it was made. Brainstorm or present common cinematic genres to help your learners with this task:

action, adventure, historical drama, horror, mystery, western, comedy, detective, love story, romantic comedy, fantasy, political drama, legal drama, satire, science fiction

Remember, the idea is not to guess the title of the film (after all this is usually seen in the sequence) but to identify the genre and how this is transmitted.

3 Get feedback from learners on the title sequences presented. Provide a sample answer where necessary, for example:

The title sequence from this Pedro Almodóvar film features vivid colours and dynamic graphics, combined with a dramatic soundtrack. All these elements highlight the comic or absurd nature of the film and anticipate the drama and intensity of the action to come. I think the film will be a comedy about …

Follow-up

Learners create their own title sequences for a real or invented film. You can create titles using Apple iMovie or Windows Movie Maker. The former includes built-in trailer templates that can be easily adapted for making title sequences. For mobile devices like iPad, try Pinnacle Studio's video editing software (pinnaclesys.com/PublicSite/uk/Products/studio/ipad).

Note

It has become popular recently for film directors to lengthen the gap between the establishing shots of a film and the title sequence. This is particularly true of films where the action and plot has to be established quickly to hook the viewer's interest, such as in James Bond or Star Trek films. Sometimes, the film's title is not revealed until the end of the film!

Variation

You could start Step 2 by presenting learners with a still screenshot from each title sequence, before playing the sequences themselves.

2   Video and narrative

Oscar-winning films are not usually known for experimenting with narrative genre. However, the opening of *Argo*, the film that won the Oscar for 2012 Best Picture, is extraordinary in the way it plays with our expectations of plot, jumping from fact to fiction. The film begins with a storyboard describing the events leading up to the 1979 Iranian revolution. You feel that you are attending a contemporary history lecture as the images are playful and cartoon-like. Then, there is grainy stock footage of rioting and protests on the streets of Tehran; you are now watching a documentary. These then combine seamlessly with the dramatic reconstruction of events. You are now watching a Hollywood suspense film. Fact or fiction? It is hard to decide in those opening minutes, but it is precisely the experimentation with narrative that captures your attention and makes you want to keep watching.

Analysing what makes a viewer keep watching is not so different from analysing what makes a language learner stay glued to the screen. Tension, curiosity, mystery and a desire to reach resolution and the end of the story are ingredients that make up a great narrative.

What I hope these activities share is that they will make learners either curious to discover the story or wish to tell their own version of events. Whether it is a funny domestic drama (Activity 2.2: *One-minute story*), the trailer for an adventure film (Activity 2.5: *Narrative errors*), a classic or contemporary love story (Activities 2.6: *Screenshot storyboard* and 2.7: *Turning points*) or a sporting event (Activity 2.9: *Penalty shoot-out*), I have chosen narrative sequences which I feel will capture a learner's attention in the same way as those first few minutes of *Argo*. The tasks themselves are designed to tap into that curiosity and to send learners off into a different world.

Video narration and Communicative Language Teaching (CLT)

Combining storytelling and video is nothing new, of course. With the arrival of the communicative approach and active viewing, using video in this way became part and parcel of classroom practice. When I first started using video in class, I recall getting learners to narrate the moving image in a number of different ways. A common task was to get Learner A facing the screen to narrate action on screen to a partner who was facing away. Learner B would then reconstruct the narrative from memory with Learner A correcting where necessary. While tasks like this were language generative, they were hard to monitor for the teacher, and learners struggled to make the narration their own. In a sense, the learners were all repeating the same kind of narration and the resolution only came for Learner B when the student checked the video him- or herself. The idea behind the tasks presented here is that the learners can provide their own narration and focus on the different ways of approaching narrative (e.g. in Activity 2.2: *One-minute story*) by highlighting the storyline, the setting, atmosphere, characters or cinematic elements. Is the story based purely on physical description or does it add extra detail or involve hypothesis?

Narration, collaboration and task types

The concept of 'live narration' which is exploited in that classic CLT jigsaw task is also explored here in a number of activities. For example, in Activity 2.2: *One-minute story*, Activity 2.8: *Be the commentator* or Activity 2.10: *Identity*. But, of course, we can now access all kinds of live events if there is an internet connection to hand, from breaking news to sports events to closed-circuit TV anywhere in the world through sites such as EarthCam (www.earthcam.com). The fact that the action is happening in real time should motivate learners to describe it vividly.

Equally motivating is getting learners into the role of an expert or real-life narrator and asking them to mimic the reactions of the narrator, whether of a sports commentator, news reporter, interviewer, narrator of a nature documentary or a judge on a music talent show. Taking on such roles adds a certain drama to proceedings, with learners getting into the role of the real-life narrator even if they are merely setting the scene of a story.

In the activities here, you'll find tried-and-tested techniques for using narrative in the language classroom. Learners predict, summarize, re-enact, reconstruct or subvert stories as before but now with the help of digital tools. In the first activity in this chapter (2.1: *See it, read it, watch it*), learners reconstruct a narrative from key words in a word cloud. In Activity 2.2: *One-minute story*, learners video their own narration of a one-minute story and identify differences in how the story is told. In Activity 2.3: *Mini Bollywood*, a digital tool is used for summarizing action by adding humorous subtitles to different scenes. Likewise, a classic task such as piecing together the key moments from a story can be done easily by taking screenshots of the scenes and then getting learners to reorder them (Activity 2.6: *Screenshot storyboard*). Finally, autobiographical information is narrated in 2.10: *Identity*, in which the learners talk about their own identity based on visual cues. The homemade quality of the video here, with its simple format and first-person narration, lends itself to be used as a stimulus for student creation.

Many of the activities emphasize the benefits of collaborative storytelling. In both Activity 2.4: *Reconstruct the plot* and Activity 2.5: *Narrative errors*, learners work together in groups to reconstruct the plot of a story in order to detect narrative errors. This seems to be fitting in the digital age where collaborative storytelling has come into its own. An example is the video storytelling competition called 'The Story Beyond the Still' which involved eight different film-makers constructing joint narratives from different still photographs (vimeo.com/groups/beyondthestill).

2.1 See it, read it, watch it

Outline	Learners reconstruct a voice-over from a word cloud.
Primary focus	Language focus: analysing and reconstructing text; predicting images from summary of text
Secondary focus	Resource: analysing relationship between image and text
Time	30–60 minutes
Level	Intermediate and above
Preparation	Find a video clip (2–5 minutes long) with a voice-over or a narrator's monologue. Ideally, there should be a number of key words embedded in the voice-over that would give clues to the visuals that accompany the narrative. Enter the text of the voice-over into an online word cloud* generator, for example Wordle (wordle.net) or Tagul (tagul.com), to create your word cloud. To increase the frequency of certain key words, you could 'doctor' the input quite simply by adding extra words to the original text.

* *Word cloud: a visual representation of text data. The more frequently the words appear in the original text, the larger they appear in the cloud. Only content words (verbs, nouns, adjectives) are included in word clouds, not function words (articles, prepositions, conjunctions, pronouns, etc.).*

Procedure

1 **See it** Show the class the word cloud you have created. Explain that the words have been taken from the voice-over of a video. The size of the words in the cloud indicates how significant they are: the larger the words, the more frequently they appear in the original text.

2 Learners attempt to find collocations or chunks in the cloud.

3 Once learners have written down some collocations, they can begin to piece together their version of the voice-over by adding function words to make full sentences. Establish a word limit and provide some background information about the clip if necessary, but not so much as to spoil the suspense of watching the film.

4 Learners compare their voice-overs in groups and choose a definitive version.

5 **Read it** Learners read out their voice-overs. Classmates then describe what they visualized while they were listening. Ask the following questions to help learners with their descriptions:

What can you visualize in the scene?
How many people do you think there are?
What other images are can you imagine?

6 Add more detail if you can.

7 Distribute or project a transcript of the original voice-over. Learners compare theirs with the original. What are the similarities and differences?

8 **Watch it** Play the video clip. Learners watch and make a note of the images. Do they coincide with images they had visualized in Step 5? Ask the following where appropriate:

What surprised you about the combination of image and text?
How is the voice-over delivered? It is dramatic, soothing, aggressive, mysterious … ?
How does that combine with the visual information?
What happens immediately after the voice-over?
What new information is revealed?

2.2 One-minute story

Outline	Learners narrate a one-minute silent video in as much detail as possible.
Primary focus	Language focus: analysing differences and similarities in the texts that emerge from the task
Secondary focus	Resource: summarizing; memorizing narrative and visual detail
Time	15–30 minutes outside class, 30 minutes in class
Level	Elementary and above
Preparation	Find a one-minute video clip with no voice-over or dialogue. The clip should be engaging and perhaps have a surprising twist at the end. Good sources are filminute.com and theoneminutes.org (check out the 'Classics' section). There are also one-minute film festivals (see oneminute.ch and filmonefest.org). For lower-level groups, choose a clip with very little action or with action that can be described using relatively simple language.

Procedure

1 Arrange for the learners to watch your selected one-minute video clip prior to class via a blog or LMS, or simply send them the link by email. Make sure that at least one learner in class does *not* see the one-minute film. If this is difficult to arrange, invite somebody into the class for Steps 4 to 8.

2 Learners watch the one-minute video as many times as they wish. When they are ready, they prepare a narration for the clip and record themselves saying it. This can be done outside class via webcam, video camera or smartphone. The narration should be between 30 and 60 seconds long and learners should try to deliver it using notes rather than simply reading a full script.

3 Learners send you their visual narratives. Upload them to a webpage (for example, tumblr.com) so that they can be easily viewed in class one after the other.

4 Play a selection of the visual narratives in class. After watching each video, learners write down any words or phrases that didn't appear in their own versions. What are the differences and similarities between their narrative and other learners' versions?

5 Get feedback from the class and identify or elicit different ways to narrate a clip. For example, some people may focus on the message behind the clip. Others may simply describe the action that is seen. Others may focus on characters or the setting. Finally, some narratives may focus on a personal response to the clip.

6 Present your own narrative for the clip and explain your approach to the task. Did you focus mainly on characters, setting, action, the message of the film?

7 At this point, the person who has *not* seen the clip summarizes the various narrations as best as he or she can. Learners can interrupt, help or correct him or her where necessary.

8 Play the clip to the whole class. The person who had not seen the clip before can discuss anything that was different from how they had imagined it.

9 Do some research into the story behind the video. How was it made? By whom? What was the intention?, etc. Provide this information as another way to narrate the video's content and meaning.

Example

Schnitzels by Tal Haring

Link: bit.ly/1bPNxEH

Possible narration

A woman is standing in a kitchen with her back to us, wearing a white dressing gown. She is hitting a piece of meat with a hammer to make it as flat as possible. A man wearing glasses is sitting at the kitchen table. He's reading a newspaper and drinking a cup of tea. Every time the woman hits the meat, the kitchen table shakes and the man's tea spills onto the table. Then, the woman suddenly stops. The man looks back at her to check she has finished hammering. He picks up the cup of tea and starts to drink it. Just as he does, the woman starts hammering again and he spills his tea onto his shirt. There's a big stain. He picks up a cloth to wipe his shirt but as he does so he knocks the cup off the table. The woman looks around. The man looks at her in a guilty way, and they stare at each other in silence. Then the man gets down on his hands and knees and picks up the pieces of broken cup. The woman continues hammering the meat.

Narrative styles

Focus on action: *The film starts with a close-up of a piece of meat. Someone is bashing it with a meat hammer and making a lot of noise …*

Focus on characters: *There is a middle-aged couple in a kitchen. The woman is standing, wearing a dressing gown. The man is sitting at the table …*

Focus on setting: *It's an ordinary suburban kitchen. There's a kitchen table with a newspaper and some tea on it …*

Focus on the message: *The film is a representation of the tensions of domestic life. It shows a couple who may have had an argument …*

Focus on personal/affective response: *It is a hilarious portrait of the monotony of married life but it is also very sad …*

Follow-up

Show a variety of one-minute films and use the following question to to initiate a discussion:
What makes a great one-minute video?

Note

Thanks to Jamie Keddie for the inspiration for this task.

2.3 Mini Bollywood

Outline	Learners practise dubbing and subtitling very short videos using the Bombay TV website.
Primary focus	Resource: developing a narrative from visual prompts; synchronizing the narrative to fit the images
Secondary focus	Skills practice: writing subtitles and dubbing
Time	10–30 minutes
Level	Elementary and above
Preparation	You will need access to the Bombay TV website (grapheine.com/bombaytv) and an internet connection in class.

Procedure

1   Elicit from the class anything they know about *Bollywood*. For example, where is the film industry based, what kinds of films are produced, what kind of audience do they have? Here are ten facts that you could point out:

Bollywood

- Bollywood is a name for the Indian popular film industry, but it enjoys success in many other countries around the world.
- Its name is formed from a blend of Bombay + Hollywood
- The Bollywood film industry started in 1913.
- Films are often made in Bombay/Mumbai with Hindi as the main language.
- Bollywood makes more films than Hollywood: over 1,000 per year. An estimated 3 billion people watch Bollywood films every year.
- Bollywood films are mostly musicals, and therefore include singing and dancing, as well as romance, comedy and action.
- They are often very long with most lasting for about three hours.
- Bright colours and extravagant costumes are characteristic of Bollywood films.
- Many Bollywood actors have had successful careers in Hollywood.
- Typical Bollywood plots feature family drama and often romance, and they usually have a happy ending.

From *Language Learning with Digital Video* © Cambridge University Press 2015   PHOTOCOPIABLE

---

2   Tell learners they are going to subtitle a mini Bollywood film using Bombay TV (grapheine.com/ bombaytv). Show them the website, explaining that the clips are around 30 seconds long and have space for three of four subtitles.

3 Demonstrate the task by writing a subtitled dialogue live online in front of the class (on a projected screen if available). It should take no more than a minute or two to do this. Make clear these three simple stages:

- Choose a sample clip
- Create the subtitles
- Share with friends and classmates

4 Learners work in pairs or small groups to subtitle a number of different mini Bollywood films and send them to others in the class to be viewed.

5 View a number of learners' mini Bollywood subtitles together as a class. Did any of the learners choose the same films? What were the similarities and differences in the subtitles? Which were the funniest?

Follow-up
After the subtitling activity, you could show the class how to dub a mini Bollywood film. This can be done on the same Bombay TV website, using the same clip you used for Step 3.

Variation
A second Bombay TV link (grapheine.com/bombaytv/v2) will take you to a drag and drop option for clips of classic film sequences (Classik TV) and football matches (Futebol TV).

Note
Thanks to Nicky Hockly for drawing my attention to this website.

2.4 Reconstruct the plot

Outline	In groups, learners build up the plot from watching a trailer.
Primary focus	Language focus: narrative tenses; sequencers
Secondary focus	Skills practice: building a sequence of narrative events from visual clues; hypothesizing; asking questions to the teacher
Time	30 minutes
Level	Pre-intermediate and above
Preparation	Find a trailer (2–3 minutes long) for a film or TV programme. The trailer should give enough visual and/or narrative information with regard to main characters, setting, plot and genre. *Important*: Make sure the film is unknown to your learners, but that you know the plot well so learners can ask you any questions about it. You will also need a short description of the plot to present to learners at the end of the class.

Procedure

1 Brainstorm and/or elicit from the learners the aim of a trailer. See Activity 3.6: *The art of the trailer* for more complete definitions of a trailer.

2 Play your selected trailer with the sound off. Pause the video occasionally to give learners time to write notes. In pairs or small groups, learners make notes under the following headings:

Genre: *romance, thriller, fantasy, comedy, etc.*
Main characters: *How many? gender, age, occupation, relationships*
Setting or settings: *How many? name of place, time of year, etc.*
Main events: *How many? What type? love scene, chase, accident, etc.*

3 Get feedback from learners. Allow them to give their opinion about the possible plot, but do not confirm or deny any suggestions at this stage.

4 Play the trailer again but this time with the sound on. In pairs or small groups, learners revise their notes to match the new information received. Their job is now to order the main events seen in the trailer into a possible plot sequence. Give the class plenty of time to do this.

5 In groups, learners then take it in turns to give their predictions about the plot, starting with the genre, characters and setting before moving on to describe the main events. After each prediction, say 'cold', 'warm' or 'hot', depending on how close each suggestion is. Again, leave plenty of time for this stage.

6 The group with the plot that most approximates the real one can then narrate their version.

7 Hand out or project the plot overview of the film so that learners can check their answers.

Variation 1
Instead of Step 7, ask the class to watch the whole film at home and come back to class to describe the differences and similarities between their version and the real thing.

Variation 2

If some of your learners are familiar with your selected film, divide the class into two groups – those who have seen the film (Group A) and those who have not (Group B). Arrange for Group A to do something else while Group B does the plot prediction task in Step 4. Learners from Group B then tell their plot reconstructions to learners in Group A, who correct them accordingly. This variation works nicely because it involves greater interaction between learners.

2.5 Narrative errors

Outline	Learners identify narrative errors in descriptions of film trailers or short video clips.
Primary focus	Language focus: predicting and correcting narrative information
Secondary focus	Skills practice: narrating scene descriptions and identifying phrases
Time	30 minutes
Level	Intermediate and above
Preparation	Find a trailer or clip (2–3 minutes long) which includes a few different scenes and chunks of dialogue. For lower-level learners, select a film that is known to the class. Prepare a few short scene descriptions from the clip (see Step 5 and the example below). *Tip*: Trailers from the 1950s and 1960s are good choices because they include fewer cuts and feature longer chunks of dialogue.

Procedure

1 Show the class a still image or a film poster of your selected trailer or clip, in which the main characters are featured. Elicit responses from the class about the film's genre or any other information about it, for example its date or the names of the film stars.

2 Show or dictate six to eight chunks of dialogue, some from the trailer or clip plus a few distractors which don't appear in the clip. Check understanding of these phrases.

3 Play the trailer or clip once only. Learners tick which lines of dialogue are actually said in the clip. They also note which characters say them.

4 Play the trailer or clip once again to check answers.

5 Present the brief scene descriptions you prepared earlier (between four and eight). Again, include some which are correct and some which have small factual errors.

6 As in Step 3, learners watch the clip and identify which descriptions are accurate and which order the correct descriptions should be in.

7 Play the trailer or clip once again to check answers.

Follow-up

Learners can choose their own clips or trailers and design the same activity at home and bring them to the next class.

Variation

Learners can correct errors in a written or a spoken synopsis of the clip or trailer.

Note

Thanks to Steve Muir for the original idea for this task.

Example

The African Queen

Link: www.tcm.com/mediaroom/video/66114/African-Queen-The-Original-Trailer-.html

This trailer is a good example because the chunks of dialogue between the two main characters are interspersed with a voice-over describing the action of the film. This gives the learners time to pause and check their answers.

Scene descriptions
Which of these scenes appear in the trailer?

1　A man embraces a woman.
2　Elephants jump into a river. (incorrect – they are crocodiles)
3　A boat is on fire. (incorrect – the building and the jungle are on fire)
4　A boat struggles to stay afloat on the rapids.
5　A man has an argument with a woman.
6　Some men shoot at the boat.

2.6 Screenshot storyboard

Outline	Learners create a storyboard (in this case, about a meeting).
Primary focus	Skills practice: narrating scene descriptions; caption writing
Secondary focus	Language focus: past narrative tenses (for Variation: present narrative tenses)
Time	30 minutes
Level	Elementary and above
Preparation	Find a video scene involving an important meeting or encounter. A good example is the meeting scene in the classic film *Brief Encounter* (1945) from 00.05.00 to 00.08.40. Prepare your own screenshot storyboard as an example (see Step 2).

Procedure

1 Learners brainstorm different ways of meeting people. Elicit some ways (e.g. through friends, blind date, online) and places (e.g. on holiday, at a conference, at a party, in a café). Learners then consider different ways to start a conversation. Elicit some classic lines (e.g. *Nice to meet you. Do you come here often?*). Find out whether the classic lines are similar to ones used in the students' own languages.

2 Show an example of a screenshot storyboard in class to establish the idea of identifying key moments in a story and creating a storyboard with screenshots. (You can make your own by following Steps 3 and 4 below.)

3 At home, learners select a scene from a film or TV series which tells the story of two people meeting. Ideally, it should be no more than three minutes long and involve some kind of build-up to the meeting. Learners select eight to ten still images from the clip to create a storyboard. They can pause the clip at key moments and take screenshots to create the storyboard images. They could also use a tool like Storybird (storybird.com/books) to make a digital story with captions.

4 Learners write short captions for each image using past tenses (past simple / past continuous). Provide model captions where appropriate (e.g. *They were studying at the same university when they met.*) to help learners build up a narrative.

5 In class, learners show or project their screenshot storyboards, narrating the different scenes from memory. Alternatively, they may play their clip with the sound off in class and read their narratives as voice-overs, trying to synchronize their narration with the clip's images.

6 They should pause the video where necessary to allow other learners to guess what is going to happen in the next screenshot, for example, how the people will meet and what the outcome of the meeting will be.

7 Learners watch and comment on each presentation. Elicit reactions from the class to these questions:

Which is the funniest meeting?
Which is the most memorable / unusual / unexpected meeting? Why?
What do you think the dialogue will be in each scene?

8 Finally, show a selection of clips with the sound on so the class can hear the original dialogue and compare with their predictions.

Note
You can use a topic other than meetings/encounters for this task, but you will need to redesign the brainstorming tasks in Step 1 to match the scene of your choice.

Variation
Instead of learners narrating the action in the past, they can comment on the screenshots using the present tenses: e.g. *He's really upset here because she's just told him that she wants to break up.*

2.7 Turning points

Outline	Learners identify key moments / turning points in a video and use them to summarize the narrative.
Primary focus	Skills practice: summarizing a narrative
Secondary focus	Language focus: key expressions for summarizing and supposition
Time	30 minutes
Level	Pre-intermediate and above
Preparation	Choose a short narrative clip that could be summarized with up to 12 stills. *Important*: The clips should include clear moments when the story changes direction, perhaps unexpectedly. Dramatic or unusual events with little or no dialogue work well, for example, a chase, an accident, a meeting, etc. See the example lesson based on *A Thousand Words*, which is available on the Cambridge University Press ELT YouTube channel (bit.ly/CUPDigitalVideo).

Procedure

1 Show the class your selected film clip without giving any information about it beforehand.

2 After watching, ask the following four questions to elicit a quick summary of the action:

Where does the action take place?
How many people are involved?
What kind of story is it?
What are the (1) key moments and (2) turning points in the story?

3 Learners compare notes and discuss which images or scenes represent the key moments and turning points in the story. Do they agree about these scenes?

4 Show the clip again. Do the learners still agree on the images that represent the above? If not, they should reach a consensus on the new key moments and turning points. There should be a maximum of six key moments and six turning points per clip.

5 In groups, learners take it in turns to describe or project the key moments and turning points. These should provide the structure to their summary. The idea is to sequence the key moments and turning points so they combine to form a single summary of the clip. *Note*: Learners can give the time references for the stills / screenshots.

6 Get feedback from the whole class. Which summary was the most accurate?

7 Ask learners: *What plot information is assumed from the clip but unsaid?* (see the 'Assumptions' section on page 54).

8 Finish by asking learners to imagine their own ending to the story.

Example

A Thousand Words

Link: Cambridge University Press ELT YouTube channel (bit.ly/CUPDigitalVideo)

Summary of key moments (in normal font) **and turning points** (*in italics*)
The cyclist sees the photographer on the train (1), the photographer has lots of luggage with her (2). She gets off the train. *The cyclist sees that she has left a camera on the seat* (3). At home, he looks at the photos on the camera (4). He sees that she is going to live in Boston (5)*. He finds a photograph that she took of him asleep on the train* (6). *He finds a photograph of her with a building in the background* (7). He goes by bicycle to the house where he thinks that photo was taken (8). *He arrives and finds a man decorating an empty apartment* (9). He decides to take a photo of himself holding his telephone number (10). *He puts the camera in a package addressed to her with 'please forward'* (11). *He waits* (12) …

Key moments

Figure 2.1: Scenes from A Thousand Words

Assumptions about *A Thousand Words*

We assume that …
… the action takes place in Los Angeles..
… she likes him.
… she leaves the camera on the train on purpose.
… the building in the background of one of the photos enables him to identify the apartment where she lives.
… he arrives too late at the apartment.
… she has already left for Boston.
… he leaves the packet with her camera in the postbox of her apartment.
… the packet will get to her eventually in Boston.
… the love story will continue …

2.8 Be the commentator

Outline	Learners narrate an exciting, fast-paced sports event as it happens in real time.
Primary focus	Skills practice: narrating actions in present tenses; describing atmosphere
Secondary focus	Language focus: present tenses; descriptive language of tension
Time	30 minutes
Level	Intermediate and above
Preparation	You will need a video clip (2–3 minutes long) of an exciting and famous sports event, plus a transcript of the accompanying commentary. A good example is *The Miracle on Ice* (1980), in which the US ice hockey team beat long-time rivals, the Soviet Union, against all the odds (youtu.be/8gfD134ED54).

Procedure

1 Show the class your selected sports event video with the sound off. If the sports event is famous but a few years old, it's unlikely that the class will know it. Ask the learners the following questions:

What is the sport? Who is playing? What is the event?
Why do you think this sports event was so important?
What do you think the commentator is saying?

2 Get feedback from the class and model answers where necessary. Explain or elicit that the job of the commentator is to describe both the action and the atmosphere in the stadium, to make it even more exciting for the viewers.

3 Show the learners the transcript of the commentary, explaining some of the background to the event.

4 Learners list elements that make the commentary exciting (e.g. use of dramatic expressions and exclamations, describing the crowd, a countdown, etc.). They can take it in turns to read out the commentary and consider where the commentator might place the intonation or raise his/her voice.

5 Play the clip again without sound so the learners can check their ideas.

6 Learners rehearse their own version of the commentary in groups. Remind the class that they can add or adapt any information they like – it doesn't matter if they know the names of the players or not – but they should try to describe the situation in as dramatic and passionate a way as possible.

7 Organize the learners in a large semi-circle. They take it in turns to read out 20-second sections of the commentary to accompany the video action. This can be done from notes or narrated from memory.

8 Play the sports event video with original audio commentary so learners can compare their versions.

Follow-up

Ask learners to bring their own video clips of great sporting moments. They can take it in turns to provide the commentary to them.

2.9 Penalty shoot-out

Outline	Learners narrate a football penalty shoot-out or the build-up to a sporting event as it happens in real time.
Primary focus	Skills practice: narrating actions in present; describing atmosphere
Secondary focus	Language focus: present tenses; descriptive language of tension
Time	30 minutes
Level	Intermediate and above
Preparation	Find a video of a penalty shoot-out. One with several minutes of build-up to the action and then commentary during and after is ideal. Another idea is to use a clip with commentary in a language not known to the learners. If played quietly, the learners can dub over the top but pick up on things like intonation and emphasis.

Procedure

1   Elicit from the class what makes a penalty shoot-out an exciting event to watch. Do the learners like watching them or not? Are they fair?

2   Show a screenshot from your selected penalty shoot-out clip prior to playing it. If it comes from a well-known match, elicit from the class possible answers to these questions (it doesn't matter if their answers are wrong):

What is the competition?
What are the two teams?
Which team is going to win?

3   Pre-teach some key vocabulary connected with the context (e.g. *to take / miss / score / save a penalty, to place the ball on the spot,* etc.) as well as verbs to describe the fans' behaviour, such as *cheer, boo, clap.*

4   Play the penalty shoot-out clip with the sound off or with foreign language commentary. Model doing a voice-over, i.e. speaking over the top of the action: '*X is coming up to take the first penalty kick. The crowd is waiting anxiously. Some people have turned their backs, they cannot look.*' Try to include a mixture of present tenses in the commentary.

5   Start playing the penalty shoot-out a second time. In pairs or small groups, the learners then begin to narrate the action. Monitor to check learners are keeping up with the action.

6   Depending on the level of your class, pause the action from time to time. Go round the class and monitor again. Make any corrections or give feedback where necessary. Make sure that the learners focus not just on the action, but also on the environment, facial expressions, atmosphere, sounds, emotions, etc. Also encourage learners to emphasize parts of their commentary to add drama.

7   Finally, watch the penalty shoot-out again as a class. Ask learners in pairs or small groups to take it in turns to narrate the action. Pay particular attention to intonation and emphasis in the narrations, the object being to make the commentary as exciting as the shoot-out itself.

Variation

Instead of a penalty shoot-out, you could use a different sporting event, such as the build-up to a sprint race. A good source for clips is the official Olympic channel on YouTube (youtube.com/user/olympic). A clip such as Usain Bolt's victory in the 100 metres sprint final at the 2012 Olympics works well (youtu.be/2O7K-8G2nwU).

Follow-up

Once learners have narrated one or two penalty shoot-outs, you could ask them to narrate part of a clip called *Refait* (vimeo.com/9426271). This film cleverly recreates the 1982 World Cup semi-final between France and Germany using two screens: on the left-hand screen is the original footage of the shoot-out. On the right-hand screen, the penalty kicks have been recreated in different urban contexts, such as a park, a tunnel and a tennis court. Learners can take turns narrating what is happening on each of the screens.

2.10 Identity

Outline	Learners analyse a video about identity and narrate their own version.
Primary focus	Stimulus: discussing the nature of identity and how this can be represented visually
Secondary focus	Language focus: language of representation (e.g. *symbolizes/stands for*) and deduction (e.g. *he could be ...*)
Time	30–60 minutes
Level	Intermediate and above
Preparation	This activity refers to a particular video clip *Identity Box* (youtu.be/amWYt9TxbHE). However, you could use any video which describes a person's identity using objects, such as a video of photos in a scrapbook. You will also need to create your own 'identity box' (see Step 1).

Procedure

1 Start with an image of your own 'identity box' and flash it up for 30 seconds. Your identity box should contain around ten pictures or objects which say something important about you.

2 Once you've removed the image from view, learners see how many items they can remember. Ask the learners: *What do these items tell you about me?* The learners hypothesise on the meanings of the objects. For example: *You chose a guitar because it's your favourite instrument.*

3 Explain the meanings behind your chosen objects. Were the learners' ideas similar?

4 Show learners the *Identity Box* video (see 'Preparation' above), or another identity-based video that you have found.

5 Learners try to recall as many objects as possible from the clip and what they represent.

6 Play the video again for learners to check their ideas. Point out the language used to refer to the objects (e.g. *X represents ..., Y stands for ...*). You could introduce other synonyms here (e.g. *convey, encapsulate, symbolize, signify*), depending on the level of your learners.

7 Learners think of ten things that they would include in their own identity box. Suggest different tools/techniques that they could use to prepare their own biographic video or multi-modal text. For example, learners could:

   - gather physical items together and film them, as in the example *Identity Box* video. The camera should focus in on different objects one by one as they are referred to in the voice-over.
   - describe their chosen items in the form of a slideshow of still images, using a tool such as VoiceThread.
   - use still images to create an 'Identity poster', or use a multi-media tool such as Glogster.

8 At home, learners make their biographic video or multi-modal text. These videos should be approximately two minutes long. They can record a voice-over, although it may be more productive for them to narrate the clip in class (see Step 9).

9 Learners project their videos/texts in class. Encourage them to perform the voice-over narration live, if possible, and to include the language items presented in Step 6.

10 Learners discuss their favourite videos/texts and any objects/images that appeared in more than one presentation.

Variation

If you don't have the facilities to project learners' videos in class, learners could simply bring in the actual objects or print out photos of them to show classmates.

Follow-up 1

Learners can watch other videos related to identity, for example: *So, Where's Home? A Film about Third Culture Kid Identity* (vimeo.com/41264088). How does each film-maker represent his or her identity? Which films do the learners like best? Why?

Follow-up 2

There are many other ways to narrate one's identity online. For example, 'Draw My Life' videos are currently a popular internet meme. Shot in fast-motion photography, they consist of a person drawing figures on a whiteboard. These figures represent people and events in the person's life, while the voice-over narration goes into more detail. Video blogger Ryan Higa's Draw My Life has been seen more than 15 million times (youtu.be/KPmoDYayoLE). Draw My Life videos are an excellent resource for the language classroom, as learners can practise the narration themselves with the original sound off. They can then make their own versions with Draw My Life video apps.

3 Video and persuasion

Advertising has always been a popular language learning resource. Video adverts are short and can be reviewed on a number of occasions in class. They often include an element of surprise and are excellent for hypothesizing as learners have seen so many before. It is possibly the genre about which our learners are most visually literate. As such, they can analyse adverts easily and use this analysis as a basis for their own creations.

However, in the digital world, notions of advertising are changing. Companies use different channels to advertise and new genres have emerged which are a combination of advertising and editorial ('advertorials'). For example, one of the most watched advertorials on YouTube in recent years was an advert disguised as a 'how-to' clip. The video *How to Shave your Body Hair* used animation and generated a high number of views. However, the advert was sponsored by Gillette, and was therefore a means of reinforcing a message about the company's shaving products but in a disguised way, as if the viewer were merely taking in 'useful information'.

The Gillette advert is an interesting example of a new genre, but one that may not be suitable for all language classrooms. On the other hand, Coca-Cola's campaign *Let's Look at the World a Little Differently* (youtu.be/ssL8r1pJe_w), which included acts of kindness and bravery recorded incidentally on security cameras around the world, proved incredibly popular in the classroom. It was successful because it tapped into the YouTube genre perfectly. It included very short clips of real people captured by accident and sandwiched together to create a good-time video with a light, upbeat message: perfect for sharing in social media networks.

Another interesting development is that the line between professionally made and amateur adverts is blurring. Companies are thus quick to pick up on any viral videos and make use of them. One of the first was a Chicken McNuggets rap that was found on YouTube and exploited by McDonald's for their own official adverts. It is not uncommon for video memes to be appropriated into the mainstream in this way.

Of course, more conventional advertising techniques are explored here as well – most notably in Activity 3.1: *Ads A: Techniques* and Activity 3.2: *Ads B: Guidelines*, with learners deciding on the most persuasive techniques and guidelines used by advertisers, and in Activity 3.3: *Promo power*, in which learners try to piece together the voice-over of a promo via visual prompts. (For a focus on a charity campaign advert see Activity 5.2 in the Video and Topic chapter.)

Trailers and teasers

One of the most persuasive video genres of all these days is the movie trailer. Trailers have become omnipresent in digital media and gain more views on YouTube than almost any other genre, except the music video. They are fascinating to analyse, partly because they have undergone radical changes in terms of objectives and content over the years. As concentration spans have diminished, the trailer has become shorter and more dramatic and evolved into the 'teaser'. These characteristics are explored in Activity 3.6: *The art of the trailer*, Activity 3.7: *Trailers past and present* and Activity 3.8: *Blurb vs trailer*, with an exploration of one of the most interesting trailers made in recent times: the trailer for David Fincher's film *The Social Network*.

Here, the relationship between text and image is highlighted with an analysis of the differences and similarities between the written blurb and the action in the trailer. Generally, identifying differences in information in a video and a reading text (and vice versa) is a useful skill to develop as so much online video is accompanied by text of some kind. By doing so, you are truly integrating video work with other skills work.

The nature of marketing on YouTube is going through interesting changes and no more so than in the teaser. In August 2013, the film director-producer JJ Abrams released a video teaser for a mystery project. Filmed in black and white, the video featured a strange man staggering out of the ocean as a narrator intoned, 'Who is he?' and ended with a frightening image of a man with his lips sewn together – a metaphor for the secret behind the campaign.

Over 2.5 million YouTube views later, there were plenty of theories about what the teaser was persuading us to go and see. However, when all was revealed, the product, called 'S', turned out not to be 'a TV series, a prequel or sequel, a crowd-sourced online mystery, or an app. It's a book – a hardback novel.'[1] The anecdote perhaps shows that these days even the most non-digital object needs a digital treatment to persuade people to consume it.

The art of persuasion is, of course, not only evident in YouTube adverts or teasers. Wherever there is a choice, the consumer needs to be persuaded to go one way or the other. This can be equally true of such disparate genres as 'how-to' videos (as analysed in Activity 3.4: *Videojugs*) or speeches (Activity 3.5: *Views about news*). Likewise, all kinds of other people have to compete for your attention in the world of YouTube and persuade you to keep watching: from amateur English teachers to teenage video bloggers.

[1] http://nyti.ms/1ho1I5S

3.1 Ads A: Techniques

Outline	Learners analyse the techniques used in a number of adverts.
Primary focus	Stimulus: debate and discussion about the techniques used to advertise products
Secondary focus	Language focus: the language of persuasion (slogans, exaggerated language, question hooks, etc.)
Time	60 minutes plus
Level	Intermediate and above
Preparation	Find a series of adverts that employ different advertising techniques (see Step 2 for a list of these). Many older adverts use the 'before and after' technique, such as those that sell washing powder or beauty products. The following tips will help you find examples of other techniques:

Guilt: adverts involving children, charity campaigns
The camera never lies: food, cleaning products
Ask the expert: health, food, science and technology
Association of ideas: cars, travel, watches
Celebrity: fashion, perfume
Storyline: almost anything!

Procedure

1 Learners think of a recent advert that they either really liked or really disliked. In pairs, ask them to think about why it was / wasn't effective. They then explain the content of the advert to their partner and discuss the following:

The message of the advert
Its intended audience
The technique used to sell the product

2 Elicit some different techniques used by advertisers. You should establish the following ones:

Advertising techniques

Before and after	We see the effect of the product before and after it has been used.
Guilt	The advert makes the viewer feel guilty for not owning the product.
The camera never lies	The advert exaggerates the visual perfection of the product.
Ask the expert	An expert in the field gives advice about a product, granting it value or prestige.
Association of ideas	A product is associated with a concept, e.g. a Rolex watch with wealth.
Celebrity	A well-known person grants a product his / her approval and therefore a certain class or cachet.
Storyline	The advert takes the form of a story or mini-drama as a way for the public to recall the product and talk about it

From *Language Learning with Digital Video* © Cambridge University Press 2015   PHOTOCOPIABLE

---

3   To help learners engage with the advertising techniques listed in Step 2, give a clear example. Choose a common, generic product (e.g. a car) and think of a suitable advert. Describe the action in your advert and spell out which technique or techniques are being used, for example:

We see a video of a small, modern car with a young woman driving it round a crowded city – the car is very cute and easy to park. There is dance music on the soundtrack. There is a little story in the ad. The woman manages to park in spaces that men with bigger cars cannot. She does it without any effort at all. The slogan is 'Size matters'. The advert promotes the idea that this car is great for city life, and that it's smart, urban, sophisticated and independent, just like the driver.

Primary technique: Association of ideas
Secondary technique: Storyline

4   Ask learners to come up with and describe other car adverts using a different association of ideas, or a different advertising technique altogether.
5   Finally, play your selected adverts, each one representing a different technique if possible. Ask learners in groups to focus on each one, describing it in a similar way to the example in Step 3 and identifying the advertising technique(s) used.

Note

A great source for adverts is Ads of the World (adsoftheworld.com/media/tv). You can filter your search by selecting the media, country, region and industry that you're interested in, as well as key words or tags. You can also try bestadsontv.com or www.visiblemeasures.com/insights/charts/adage (good for viral adverts).

Variation

To familiarize the class with the techniques, find adverts with voice-overs or some form of dialogue / narration. Present transcripts of the texts to the learners, but don't show them the adverts or indicate what the product is. The learners match the texts to the techniques and predict the content of the advert. Finally, they check their answers by watching the adverts.

3.2 Ads B: Guidelines

Outline	Learners evaluate successful adverts according to guidelines.
Primary focus	Stimulus: debating and discussing guidelines used to advertise products
Secondary focus	Language focus: language of evaluation and decision-making
Time	60 minutes plus
Level	Intermediate and above
Preparation	Find a selection of award-winning adverts online. The Advertising Educational Foundation website (aef.com/exhibits/awards) lists all the main advertising awards. Follow the separate awards links and you'll find the winners in different categories. Make sure you click on 'Film'. The following link provides you with the 2010 Clio Awards winners in the category of film: aef.com/exhibits/awards/clio_awards/2010/01 (see the example below).

Procedure

1   Elicit from learners what they think makes a good video advert. Perhaps ask one or two people to suggest one they have seen and reasons why it is successful.
2   Establish guidelines 1–10 below and ask learners to match them with descriptions a–j. Allow learners to add further guidelines if they wish to.

Advertising guidelines

1   Humour
2   Novelty / Element of surprise
3   Script
4   Soundtrack
5   Emotional pull
6   Call to action
7   Story
8   Simplicity
9   Credibility / Empathy
10 Late product identification

a   Something attracts you to the advert because it is original or unexpected.
b   This delaying technique makes you curious about what the product is.
c   The message should not be too complicated.
d   The text which complements the image can convey a powerful message.
e   Music can enhance the product's image enormously.
f   An advert that makes you laugh sticks in the mind.
g   The public's identification with a product makes it believable.
h   An advert is more memorable if you are affected by it emotionally.
i   A strong narrative is everything.
j   The advert provides new information which makes you act.

From *Language Learning with Digital Video* © Cambridge University Press 2015   PHOTOCOPIABLE

---

3 Check answers (1f, 2a, 3d, 4e, 5h, 6j, 7i, 8c, 9g, 10b). Then conduct a discussion on guidelines 1–10, asking learners to rank them in order of importance. Learners should reach a consensus where possible, but clearly there are no right answers as such.

4 Show your selection of award-winning adverts (see 'Preparation' above for sources). Learners watch each one and evaluate it according to the ten guidelines on page 65. They should consider these questions:

Which of guidelines 1–10 are exemplified in each advert? One or many?
How are they exemplified?
Are some guidelines used in several adverts? If so, which ones?
Have you changed your mind about the ranking of these guidelines now that you have seen the adverts?

5 Get feedback from different groups of learners. Find out which proved to be the class's favourite advert and establish why.

Example

Find your Greatness

Link: youtu.be/LsXRj89cWa0

Guidelines in order of importance

Novelty / Element of Surprise	The overweight 12-year-old boy in the advert is not the kind of role model that we might expect in a fitness advert for Nike.
Script	Extremely important – it carries the whole message. It says that 'greatness' is something all of us are capable of.
Emotional pull	We feel what the boy is feeling as he struggles.
Simplicity	All we see is the boy running; the whole message is in the script.
Credibility / Empathy	The advert openly invites us to empathize with the boy.
Late product identification	We have no idea what the product is until the final second. There is only an indirect connection between the product and the message.

The jogger advert was not without controversy. Some critics claimed that it was patronizing and disturbing to show a 12-year-old boy running painfully slowly along an empty road. Others claimed that it simply perpetuated the idea that slim people work hard to be slim, and are therefore superior.

Follow-up 1

Nike produced several adverts with the same *Find your Greatness* message. You can find another one here: youtu.be/_hEzW1WRFTg. Ask learners to compare the advert in this link with the award-winning jogger advert in the example on page 66. Which is more effective and why?

Follow-up 2

Role play: Pairs or groups select and present an advert as if they had created it themselves, and argue the case for it being an award winner. Other groups or pairs vote to find the most popular advert.

Note 1

It's worth pointing out that in the past adverts did not follow some of the guidelines described in this activity. Decades ago it was commonplace to produce adverts that simply named the product early on, repeated the name again and again, and even indicated where you could purchase it. The guidelines on page 66 show that advertising has since become a more sophisticated process.

Note 2

Here are links for some original adverts that are likely to engage interest and create debate in class. Remember to vet the the comments which appear below the clips before you show them to learners!
John Lewis (Christmas): youtu.be/oN8axp9nHNU and youtu.be/XqWig2WARbo
Evian (Roller Babies): youtu.be/XQcVllWpwGs
Dove (Real Beauty Sketches): youtu.be/XpaOjMXyJGk

3.3 Promo power

Outline	Learners watch a promotional (or 'promo') video and analyse the techniques that it employs.
Primary focus	Resource: identifying the characteristics of a promo video
Secondary focus	Language focus: identifying linguistic strategies of a promo video and creating a voice-over
Time	15–30 minutes
Level	Pre-intermediate and above
Preparation	Find a short promo video. *The Power of Video* is used as an example and is available on the Cambridge University Press ELT YouTube channel (bit.ly/CUPDigitalVideo). However, you could use any clip which shows how a product or service operates and what its benefits are. Other good examples would be promos for new software programs, apps or other internet services.

Procedure

1   Learners brainstorm a product or service that has been demonstrated to them recently via a video promo. Ask these questions to get learners thinking:

How long was the promo video?
Why was it in video format?
How convincing was it?
Did you buy the product or service?

If learners cannot think of a particular promo, give an example of your own, for example:

I recently saw a promo about advantages of buying a 'premium' well-known music streaming service. It was only 30 seconds long; it explained that with premium there are no adverts …

2   Tell learners they are going to watch a one-minute promo video about the medium of video itself! Ask learners to make a list of reasons why video is such an effective tool for persuading people to buy something. For example, it's fast-paced, it captures your attention, it's memorable, it conveys lots of information extremely quickly.

3   Learners watch *The Power of Video* (see 'Preparation' above) with the sound off. In pairs or small groups, the learners then attempt to create a voice-over (no more than 150 words long). The animated text used in the clip will be very useful, but you can also provide some key vocabulary or collocations from the original narration, for example:

capture attention	*online world*	*engage customers*
visual information	*purchase a product*	

4   Play the clip as many times as necessary, freeze-framing different images. Ask learners to look carefully at these, as many give clues to the content of the voice-over message. For example, you could ask: *What's the connection between a goldfish and your attention span?* (This is explained in the first ten seconds of the clip.)

5   Learners take it in turns to read out their voice-overs, synchronizing their narration with the promo's animated text where possible. Conduct feedback with the whole class and analyse the differences and similarities between the various narrations.

6 Learners now watch the promo with the sound on. How similar was their voice-over to the original? What differences did they notice? Give learners a transcript of the voice-over if necessary – see below.

The Power of Video

Link: Cambridge University Press ELT YouTube channel (bit.ly/CUPDigitalVideo)

Voice-over transcript
According to a recent study about web use, the average attention span online in 2012 was 8 seconds: somewhat shorter than that of a goldfish. Alarming if you're trying to capture an audience's attention in an otherwise noisy online world. You need content that engages your customers and quickly. If you have a story to tell, there is no better way of telling it than using the power of a video.

90% of information transmitted to the brain is visual and visuals are processed 60,000 times faster in the brain than text. In fact, viewers spend 100% more time on web pages with videos on them and 85% are more likely to purchase a product after watching a video.

Videos communicate messages quickly and simply. They entertain, impress and are more likely to be shared. You've almost reached the end of this video. Congratulations! You are better than a goldfish.

From *Language Learning with Digital Video* © Cambridge University Press 2015   PHOTOCOPIABLE

---

7 Next, learners discuss which persuasive techniques were used in *The Power of Video*. Did the promo include:

- Statistics and facts?
- Satisfied customers' comments?
- A list of impressive results or benefits?
- Familiar and/or memorable images?
- Information about competitive pricing/value?
- A combination of text and audio messages?
- A lot of information in a small amount of time?

8 Finish by asking these questions:

Is the promo as engaging and convincing as the message it is trying to transmit?
What images or facts most stick in the mind?
Who is it aimed at? How do you know?
How could the promo be improved?
Is animation the best way of communicating the message?

3.4 Videojugs

Outline	Learners brainstorm how to do a particular activity and then compare with 'how-to' videos.
Primary focus	Resource: discovering how to do something
Secondary focus	Language focus: analysing the language of instruction (e.g. sequencers, imperatives, warnings)
Time	30–60 minutes
Level	Intermediate and above
Preparation	Find two 'how-to' videos from Videojug (videojug.com) on the same subject. For the purposes of this lesson, it is good to choose a subject that not everybody in the class knows a lot about, but that is not overly complicated. The example on page 71 uses two 'how-to' videos on choosing dog breeds. You will also need transcripts of the videos. *Note:* the advantage of the Videojug site is that transcripts are available below the clips, so you can easily make these available to your learners (see Step 4).

Procedure

1   Establish the subject of the 'how-to' videos that you are going to watch in class. Elicit two or three general pieces of advice about the topic to give the learners a start. If there is an 'expert' in the class, don't allow them to dominate at this stage!

2   In groups, learners brainstorm more ideas so that they have at least five tips to share with the rest of the class.

3   Play the first 'how-to' video. Learners note the main points made in the video and see if they coincided with their own ideas.

4   Play the second 'how-to' video on the same subject. Learners again note down the main points. Ask these questions about both videos:

Which advice appears in both videos?
How is the advice different in each video?
Which visual elements help communicate the message?
Which of the 'how-to' talks is clearer? Why?
What kind of language do the speakers use in their videos?
Which of the speakers is more persuasive? Why? Is it to do with tone, manner, content?

At this point you could distribute copies of the transcripts for both 'how-to' videos. These are available on the Videojug site.

5   Learners prepare their own 'how-to' talk on the above subject, taking the best or most interesting features from each of the two talks. Encourage them to use particular features of instructional language, such as imperatives, sequencers and warnings:

First, you need to make sure that …	*The next thing you need to do is …*
Be careful that you don't …	*Always remember to …*
Don't forget to …	*Watch out for …*

You could draw up a list of these on the board before the next step.

6   Learners present their 'how-to' talks to the rest of the group.

Follow-up

At home, learners prepare a 'how-to' presentation for an activity that they know how to do well, for example cook a specific meal. In the next class, they can enact the presentation. Encourage learners to use instructional language (see Step 5). If they can do their presentation outside the class 'in situ' all the better. For example, a demonstration of a recipe could take place in a kitchen.

Example

Videojug 1: *How to choose a dog*

Link: videojug.com/film/how-to-choose-a-dog

Content

The video is organised clearly and coherently, consisting of an introduction, five steps and a conclusion. The five steps are: 1) Assess the need, 2) Consider activity and space, 3) Budget, 4) Choose the breed, age and sex, 5) Make a connection.

Characteristics of the script

- Direct questions to the viewer: *Will it be for companionship? Security?*
- Imperatives : *Consider a few things … Assess the need...*
- Conditionals: *If you have limited space … If your schedule …*
- Informal tone: *What it all comes down to is this …*
- Reference to other experts: *According to pet experts …*

Visual aspects

We don't see the presenter at all, just images of different dogs and their owners, edited so that these images usually coincide with the content of the script. Intertitles and numbers on screen indicate the five steps.

Videojug 2: *How to choose a dog breed*

Link: videojug.com/film/how-to-choose-a-dog-breed

Content

The presenter here makes many of the same points as the presenter of Video 1, referring to cost, time, space, size, etc. However, the presenter uses longer sentences and is generally more vague. The overall message is 'do a lot of research before you buy', which is less practical than the messages in Video 1.

Characteristics of the script

Many language features are similar to those used in Video 1, such as imperatives, conditionals and direct questions (e.g. *How big is your house?*).

Visual aspects

We mainly see the presenter giving information from his veterinary clinic. There are no intertitles to highlight the points made, and virtually no images of dogs, so it is generally harder to recall what is said about them.

3.5 Views about news

Outline	Learners watch two talks about news coverage and decide which is the most persuasive.
Primary focus	Resource: learners discover information about news coverage
Secondary focus	Stimulus: discussing the news today and its impact on our lives; ranking the performance of a public speaker
Time	30–45 minutes
Level	Upper intermediate and above
Preparation	Find two short talks on a similar subject, each no more than 5 minutes in length. This activity has been designed around two TED.com* talks about the news:

1 *The News about the News*:
   ted.com/talks/alisa_miller_shares_the_news_about_the _news
2 *And Now the Real News*:
   ted.com/talks/kirk_citron_and_now_the_real_news
   However, any two talks could be used to rank persuasiveness (see Variations).

* TED.com provide a rich source of information on contemporary subjects. Its talks are ideal for classroom use and self-study as they include subtitles in many languages and a trackable transcript.

Procedure

1 Elicit what kinds of news stories your learners receive every day and how they receive them. How has this changed recently? Use the following prompts to help discussion:

News

Type of news	personal, local, international, current affairs, sports, trivia, gossip, sensationalism, entertainment, business, niche (health, technology, etc.)
Sources of news	Official news outlets: print, television, radio, Internet
	Social network updates: Facebook, Twitter, etc.
	Viral videos: YouTube, Huffington Post, Digg, etc.
	Word-of-mouth: chat, phonecalls, SMS, What's App, etc.

From *Language Learning with Digital Video* © Cambridge University Press 2015   PHOTOCOPIABLE

---

2 Elicit or establish that online video is increasingly the medium by which we access the news, and that 'citizen journalism' is increasingly prevalent because of expanding access to smartphones and fast internet connections. To a certain extent, we no longer go to the news, the news comes to us.

3 Play the two TED talks. Learners match sentences a– h on page 73 to either Talk 1: *The News about the News* or Talk 2: *And Now the Real News*.

a   People can't find a connection with the news because it is not made relevant to their context.
b   There is too much news.
c   News coverage is biased towards local, not international, stories.
d   We don't know much about the world now because of the type of news coverage.
e   The news we receive is too superficial.
f   All news is recycled from the same sources.
g   News stories should be about issues that will matter 50 years from now.
h   Science can provide us with more profound news.

Answers: Talk 1 = c, d, e, f; Talk 2 = a, b, g, h.

4   Check answers with the whole class. Then ask learners to think about the nature of the talks themselves. How are they different? What do they have in common? Learners answer these questions:

How are the talks structured?
How do the talks begin and end?
What type of news is described?
How is each specific news item presented?
Are statistics / facts presented?
Are images / maps / graphs used?
What is the presenters' style like? (tone of voice, body language etc.)
How does the audience react?

5   Learners discuss the above questions in groups. Conduct feedback with the whole class, then refer learners to the comments section below each talk. Do any comments reinforce the learners' notes and opinions?
6   Learners now vote on the best talk. Did they reach a consensus? How could the talks be more persuasive?

Variation 1
Politicians: Do the same task for two politicians, using speeches or party political broadcasts. What techniques are used to convince the electorate how to vote? Which campaign is the most persuasive? Why? (Try americanrhetoric.com for a great range of speeches from different genres.)

Variation 2
Same news, different coverage: Find two news video broadcasts on the same topic. Make sure they are substantially different in their coverage in terms of the information given, the reporting angle and narrative style. Learners identify the differences and decide which is the most persuasive and/or informative report.

3.6 The art of the trailer

Outline	Learners analyse various film trailers.
Primary focus	Resource: describing trailers and discussing their characteristics
Secondary focus	Language focus: language of description (*there is / are … it includes … x is mentioned …*)
Time	30–60 minutes
Level	Intermediate and above
Preparation	You will need two or three different film trailers. A good site to access trailers is Trailer Addict (traileraddict.com). Also, the Key Art Awards announces the 'Best Trailers of the Year' (keyartaward.com).

Procedure

1 Elicit from learners or explain what the aim of a trailer is. Provide the list below and ask learners to say which they feel is the best definition:

   a   to provide a summary of the film's content
   b   to show the audience what makes this film unique
   c   to reveal just enough of a film to make an audience want to go and see it
   d   to show the best moments or highlights of a film
   e   to raise interest and ask provocative questions about the film

2 Elicit and / or present these 12 typical characteristics of trailers:

Characteristics of trailers

1   The name of the film is mentioned at the end.
2   There are close-ups of the main actors.
3   Dramatic music is included.
4   There are a large number of fast cuts.
5   Key words, a slogan, a catchphrase or captions situate you in the place and time of the movie.
6   Key dramatic moments from the film are included.
7   There is a dramatic change of pace or direction.
8   There are short extracts of dialogue and other soundbites.
9   Characters, setting and plot are all established to an extent.
10 There is an unresolved conflict, argument or problem.
11 A narrator describes or summarizes the film in an exaggerated tone.
12 Written quotes 'sell' the movie with superlatives and other exclamations.

From *Language Learning with Digital Video* © Cambridge University Press 2015   PHOTOCOPIABLE

---

3 Show your selected trailers (see examples on pages 75 and 76), asking learners to decide which of the 12 characteristics apply to each one.

4 Play the trailers again so that learners can check their answers. Get feedback from the whole class and provide or elicit particular examples of the characteristics. For example, you could refer to certain key words or describe particularly memorable images.

5 Discuss with the class which of the trailers they prefer or which is more 'special', and why.

6 Discuss, too, what learners have found out about the plots and the characters from seeing the trailers. What questions does a particular trailer raise? Would it make them go and see the film?

Follow-up

(For higher levels) Learners choose a film they know well, and without seeing the original trailer they design their own version, selecting some of the features from the list in Step 2 on page 74. There are obviously too many cuts to create an exact storyboard, but learners can describe certain scenes or quotations that they would like to include.

Example

Trailer 1: *The Social Network*

Link: thesocialnetwork-movie.com

Typical characteristics included (see Step 2 on page 74)

1 The name of the film appears right at the end.

4 Nearly 100 cuts in 2.5 minutes

5 Captions give the time and location, plus an indication of the storyline.

6 There are lots of arguments, there is a fire.

7 The first minute is very different from the rest, showing different people keying in information on Facebook. The rest of the trailer is more conventional, showing highlights and climactic moments from the film.

8 There are lots of different soundbites and dialogue extracts, some as voice-overs and some where we see the characters speaking.

9 We know where and when the film takes place. The atmosphere is established, we understand who the main characters are and something of the conflict between them. We get a clear idea that the film is a dramatized history about the inventors of Facebook.

10 There is an argument between what seem to be the two main characters, in which other people are also involved. The final scene seems to be a court case or a disciplinary board.

Special characteristics
Rather than dramatic music, there is a quiet song running in the background which doesn't appear in the movie. There is an element of humour at the end, both in the captions and in the final quotation. It has a very quiet opening and ending, not at all typical of trailers.

Trailer 2: *The African Queen*

Link: www.tcm.com/mediaroom/video/66114/African-Queen-The-Original-Trailer-.html

Typical characteristics included (see Step 2 on page 74)

2 Close-ups of the two main actors Humphrey Bogart and Katharine Hepburn make up a good part of the trailer. They were big-name movie stars at the time.

3 Music is included to emphasize the most dramatic moments. Sound effects such as animal noises are also used to this effect. However, the music is light-hearted which seems to run contrary to the high drama.

6 We see crocodiles, an attack. The boat almost sinking in the rapids, etc.

8 Climactic moments of conversation are shown, always with the characters in view.

9 The background of the movie is explained.

10 We see arguments between Bogart and Hepburn. They appear to have very different characters.

11 The narrator describes a good part of the plot as well as summarizing the personalities of the two main characters. The tone is exaggerated, using promotional language from that time, including positive adjectives, superlatives, etc.

12 Exclamations and claims are flashed up on screen, for example: 'Never before has the screen combined such talent and artistry …'.

Interestingly, the trailer doesn't include the title of the movie at the end, but at the beginning.

3.7 Trailers past and present

Outline	Learners analyse different film trailers from a historical perspective.
Primary focus	Resource: discussing the differences between trailers past and present
Secondary focus	Language focus: the language of comparison
Time	30–60 minutes
Level	Intermediate and above
Preparation	You will need a set of different film trailers from different ages. It is a good idea to do Activity 3.6: *The art of the trailer* before this activity, so that learners have a clear idea of the general characteristics of trailers. *Tip*: You can choose very well-known trailers to show to your class, but bear in mind that some of these are not typical of the genre, such as Alfred Hitchcock's *Psycho* which includes the director's own narration.

Procedure

1 Learners describe any film trailers they have seen recently and what they like / dislike about them. Where did they see them? At the cinema? Online? Will they go and see the film as a result?

2 Revise or present the 12 typical characteristics of trailers mentioned in Activity 3.6: *The art of the trailer* (see page 74). Elicit from learners what they think the difference is between trailers made in the 1950s and those made today.

3 Present learners with a trailer from the 1940s or 1950s and ask them to tick the relevant characteristics from the list in Activity 3.6 (page 74). Learners then do the same thing for a contemporary film. You could use the two example trailers in Activity 3.6 (see pages 75 and 76).

4 Get feedback from the learners on the differences and similarities between the characteristics of the two trailers. Make sure learners use a variety of phrases for making comparisons.

5 To conclude, learners summarize the three main strategies each trailer used to persuade people to watch the film, for example:

1950s: close-ups of big-name movie stars; shots of exotic locations, etc.
Present day: focus on plot and fast-paced action, etc.

3.8 Blurb vs trailer

Outline	Learners compare the written information presented in a blurb and the visual information in a trailer.
Primary focus	Resource: analysis of written and visual texts for studying persuasive language
Secondary focus	Language focus: language of persuasion
Time	30–60 minutes
Level	Intermediate and above
Preparation	You will need a written 'blurb' or promotional text about a film or TV series (these can be commonly found on the film's or series' website) and a corresponding trailer.

Procedure

1 Learners discuss different ways that they can find out about a new film, book or TV series, for example: watch a trailer online, read a review in the newspaper, read a publicity blurb about it. Which of these texts usually convince the class to watch or read the work in question?

2 Show learners a written blurb of between 100 and 150 words. Elicit, where possible, characteristics of promotional language in the text. Then help learners unpack the text, highlighting different features of persuasive language such as the ones shown here:

Persuasive language

words with positive associations (*awesome, star, brilliant*)
comparatives and superlatives (*the best, the most, better than ever*)
intensifying expressions (*highly, totally, completely, utterly*)
imperatives (*check it out, don't miss this, tell your friends*)
catchy expressions and figurative language (*a real gem! out of this world*)

From *Language Learning with Digital Video* © Cambridge University Press 2015   PHOTOCOPIABLE

---

3 Focus learners' attention on the structure of the blurb. How is the text constructed? For example, does it contain an opening sentence describing what the film is about? Does it mention the actors, director or screenwriter? Does it compare the film or TV series to something else?

4 Learners watch the trailer and compare it with the written blurb. Present these questions to the class:

Which parts of the blurb are also represented in the trailer?
Which parts of dialogue in the trailer echo the message in the blurb?
Is the theme of the film communicated more effectively through the blurb or the trailer? Why?

5 Ask learners to compare their answers and get feedback from the class.
6 Learners watch a trailer for another film and write a complementary blurb of between 100 and 150 words, using the characteristics given in Step 2.

Variation

Learners compare the voice-over used in the trailer for a film like *The African Queen* with the written blurb for *The Social Network* (see link below). *Note:* The voice-over from a 1950s trailer has, in fact, many of the characteristics of the written blurbs of today.

Example

The Social Network

Go to thesocialnetwork-movie.com to see a written blurb for the film.

Persuasive language used in the blurb
Words with positive associations: *stunning, complex, incisive, brilliant, success*
Intensifying expressions: *superbly crafted*
Catchy expressions and figurative language: *new breed, emotional brutality, unfathomable success, punk genius, spark a revolution*

Content of the blurb
The blurb includes exaggerated claims about the story and its main characters to heighten its importance, for example: *… sparked a revolution … changed the face of human interaction … rewove the fabric of society…*

---

4 Video and music

If there is one genre that has been transformed by the digital age, it is the music video. Many of today's most popular singers and groups have been discovered on sites such as YouTube. Canadian singer Justin Bieber became a superstar at the age of 15 on the basis of the songs he uploaded to the video-sharing site. Here, amateurs reign supreme: recording songs in their bedrooms one minute, and the next attracting corporate sponsors to pay for product placement in their clips or production of online adverts. Record a version of a Lady Gaga song at your college music festival and you may end up with 50 million views in a month, as did Greyson Chance (youtu.be/bxDlC7YV5is).

But it is not only the discovery of new talent in terms of performance that has transformed the music video, but the arrival of fan-made videos. *Billboard* now recognize fan-made videos that use authorized audio, as well as official promos, in the compilation of charts of the most popular online music.[1] It is yet another example of the omnipresence of 'own-created' media and how this is having an impact on, or indeed taking over, the mainstream.

However, YouTube music videos can be used for many other purposes these days. For example, the song 'Crush on Obama' (youtu.be/wKsoXHYICqU), performed by a fan of the politician, then filmed and edited by amateurs and uploaded to YouTube, was said to have played a major part in the election of the US President in 2009.

So, what are the implications of these enormous changes for the language classroom? Traditionally, music videos have been exploited in the language classroom by gap-fills based around the song's lyrics. Whilst this is a worthwhile exercise in many ways, and clearly tests students' listening skills, it does not consider the role of the video itself but rather gives priority to the text in isolation. Such activities can be done equally well with audio alone. Secondly, there are a number of online tools and sites available now (a good example is lyricstraining.com) which enable learners to do these lyric gap-fills on their own outside class. For these reasons, today's learners may find merely going through the lyrics of a song in class a little monotonous. That frees up classroom time to focus on the visual message of music videos. This is highlighted particularly in Activity 4.2: *Beyond the lyrics* where learners read the lyrics first and then have to visualize the video themselves. They then check and find out if their visualizations were similar or not to the original version. Likewise in Activity 4.8: *Performance!* learners analyse the lyrics first and then imagine how these will come alive when performed.

There are many different versions of familiar songs online and many that the learners can provide themselves. There are also musical innovations out there, in which two different songs or videos are combined in mash-ups. These innovations are specifically explored in Activities 4.3: *One song, many versions*, 4.4: *Two songs, one video* and 4.5: *Mash-up madness*.

Finally, the music video is in itself a fascinating cultural phenomenon, as revealed by an exhibition *The Art of Pop Video* which paid homage to 'this ever-evolving genre; one which is uniquely placed to instantly react to the changes in technology, and shifts in popular culture' (bit.ly/JDd9Lt). As an

---

[1] *Billboard* charts are now collated from digital sales, radio airplay and internet streaming data.

example, just compare two music videos, each over 10 minutes in length, which are films in their own right: Michael Jackson's 'Thriller' and Lady Gaga's 'Telephone'. With higher-level learners, it would be an interesting exercise to trace the history of the genre and indeed of musical scores in film in general, from Prokofiev's classical score for *Alexander Nevsky* to the eclectic songs found in Tarantino's *Pulp Fiction*. See Activities 4.1: *Listen and predict* and 4.2: *Beyond the lyrics* for a broader view of the genre.

Of course, there is more to music on film than the music video. Activity 4.1: *Listen and predict* looks at the importance of film soundtracks, with learners predicting the genre, and Activity 4.6: *Change the soundtrack* gets the learners to participate as much as possible in the selection of a soundtrack. This participation is all-important. You could also allow the class to bring in their own music videos or favourite soundtracks to help create their own 'video jukebox'.

Finally, there's performance: in Activity 4.7: *Videoke*, learners watch and perform a song at the same time in a number of ways. They can change the song as they see fit, perhaps making a literal version of it in which the lyrics actually reflect what is being seen in the video (see Variation 3 in Activity 4.7). In any case, both the relationship between text and image and the learners' participation are once again brought to the foreground here. After having a go at singing, the chapter finishes with learners analysing how a performance enhances a text in terms of rhythm, pace, intonation and body language in Activity 4.8: *Performance!*.

4.1 Listen and predict

Outline	Learners listen to music snippets of different soundtracks to predict the film genre.
Primary focus	Stimulus: using video to trigger reactions when listening to music; predicting genres
Secondary focus	Language focus: lexis of film genres and sensations; language of description
Time	10–30 minutes (depending on the number of clips you have)
Level	Pre-intermediate and above
Preparation	You will need a series of four or five different soundtrack video clips, edited together into one sequence. There are plenty available online. A selection of 30 very famous soundtracks can be found at: youtu.be/odi9tiulb4Q

Procedure

1 Introduce the concept of film soundtracks by asking the following questions:

Why is a soundtrack important?
Do you have any particular favourites?
Which well-known ones are you familiar with?

2 Brainstorm different film genres and adjectives to describe music:

Film genres:
action, comedy, romantic comedy, drama, horror, musical, romance, science fiction, thriller, etc.

Adjectives to describe music:
romantic, dynamic, exciting, moving, melodic, rhythmic, gentle, dramatic, spooky, etc.

3 Start playing your sequence of different soundtrack excerpts (see suggested source in 'Preparation' above). If playing the sequence via a computer, turn the screen off so students cannot see any accompanying films clips or images. After each excerpt, pause the sequence and present the following questions to the learners:

What type of music is it? What adjectives describe it?
What does it remind you of? What mood or atmosphere does it evoke?
What type of film do you think it comes from?
Think of a scene that this music could accompany. Who is in it? Where are they? What's going on?

4 Learners compare answers to the above and report back to whole class. Make sure to get different opinions from the class where possible.
5 Play the different soundtrack excerpts again, but this time with all film clips and images revealed. Were there any surprises? Which music was the easiest or the most difficult to identify, in terms of film genre?

Note 1
The activity works best with music-only soundtracks (i.e. no vocal track as you would have with James Bond songs, for example). Bear in mind the age of the films in question and whether the learners are familiar with the clips. It is sometimes better to choose less well-known films so that the learners are forced to guess the genre. However, see Variation 2 for working with well-known films. The most instantly recognizable musical scores include *Psycho, 2001: A Space Odyssey, The Godfather, Jaws, Schindler's List, Titanic, Star Wars* and *Mission Impossible*.

Note 2
Songs in the Cinema: In the 1960s, the lyrics of songs were used to comment on a situation or reveal a character's feelings in a film, for example, Paul Simon's songs in *The Graduate*. If you wanted to focus on particular songs and how they are represented in the cinema, well-known films include *Pulp Fiction, Trainspotting, Saturday Night Fever, Superfly* and *Help*.

Variation 1
To make the task considerably easier, you could present the students with the names of the films and ask the learners to match them with the soundtracks.

Variation 2
You could use famous soundtracks which you feel will be known to the majority of learners (such as the one for the film *Jaws*) and ask learners to visualize the scene or describe what they see in their mind's eye as they hear the music. See 'Note 1' above for other well-known musical scores.

Variation 3
Sounds: Instead of using music, select a clip with some interesting sound effects and ask learners to predict the scene. Priming the class with some questions should help with the visualization, for example: *Is it outside or inside? How do you know? How many people are there?*

4.2 Beyond the lyrics

Outline	Learners design a video around a song.
Primary focus	Stimulus: identifying the message of a music video and how this can be portrayed visually
Secondary focus	Language focus: language of hypothesis; narration of action
Time	30–60 minutes
Level	Intermediate and above
Preparation	Choose a music video whose action enhances or transcends the song lyrics or where the images reflect the sentiment of the song. It should *not* be a straight performance of the song. You will also need access to the lyrics of the song. Classics include Bob Dylan's 'Subterranean Homesick Blues', Peter Gabriel's 'Sledgehammer', Michael Jackson's 'Thriller', Pink Floyd's 'Another Brick in the Wall', REM's 'Everybody Hurts' (see example below), Bjork's 'All Is full of Love', Lady Gaga's 'Telephone' and Kylie Minogue's 'Come into my World'. *Tip*: Don't choose a contemporary music video which everyone has seen. It's better to choose one which is well-known, but not from the present day.

Procedure

1 Distribute or project the lyrics of your selected song and ask learners to read them. Clarify any unknown words or expressions. Present the class with the following questions:

What do you think the theme of the song or its main message is?
What images spring to mind when you read the lyrics?

2 Learners then work in pairs or groups to choose what type of music video they would make to accompany the lyrics. Ask them to choose a basic framework from the options below, and to explain their choice:

a A mini drama in which the singer(s) appears performing the song.
b A narrative or a drama with the song as the soundtrack but with no actual performance of the song.
c A narrative or drama which is interrupted at some point by the singer's performance.

3 Explain or elicit what a storyboard for a video is and how it summarizes the main events in a video. If possible, show the learners some examples of music storyboards (you can find plenty of examples by searching online for 'music video storyboards'). In small groups, learners then create a storyboard for their video, adding the relevant lyrics below each frame/still image. There should be no more than ten frames/still images altogether. Learners could use PowerPoint or another storytelling software tool (e.g. VoiceThread) to create the storyboard, or it could be done by hand.

4 Each group of learners plays the song in class, pausing the music to explain the scene or action in each of their storyboard frames. Learners should describe each frame in as much detail as possible. For example:

At the start of the song, the band members are walking across an open field. It's a very big, flat field and they are very small, black figures surrounded by this empty landscape. When the chorus begins we see the lead singer on top of a mountain …

5 Learners listen and watch each other's storyboard commentaries and choose their favourite.
6 Finally, show the original music video to the learners. Elicit impressions from them about the differences and similarities between the original and their own work.

Follow-up
Learners choose their own song and prepare their music video storyboards in a similar way at home. They then present their work in the next class.

Example

'Everybody Hurts' by REM

Link for lyrics: lyricsmode.com/lyrics/r/rem/everybody_hurts.html

Link for video: youtu.be/ijZRClrTgQc

What do you think the theme of the song or its main message is?
Loneliness, alienation, feeling sad, empathy, recovery.

What images spring to mind when you hear the lyrics?
People looking sad and alone, perhaps in a big city, but then people in groups, hugging each other, making each other feel better.

What kind of music video would you make to accompany the lyrics?
A narrative or a drama with the song as the soundtrack but with no actual performance of the song. It's a sad song so images will probably be more meaningful than just watching the band sing.

Describe your storyboard frame by frame:
The video starts with lots of people going to work, crowded underground trains, people looking stressed …
The faces are all blurred … We want to show how the city can be a lonely, alienating place …

4.3 One song, many versions

Outline	Learners compare different versions of the same song.
Primary focus	Stimulus: identifying differences between interpretations of a song and how these are represented visually
Secondary focus	Language focus: language of comparison; lexis of musical genres
Time	30–60 minutes
Level	Intermediate and above
Preparation	Choose a song that has many cover versions available on video. The example on page 88 is based around the song 'I Will Survive'. It's a good idea to choose cover versions where the performance style shifts significantly from the original, such as a rap version of a ballad. For example, compare Pink's original version of 'Perfect' (youtu.be/K3GkSo3ujSY) with Ahmir's cover version (youtu.be/gliHyklHr6c).

Procedure

1 Introduce the concept of cover versions by asking these questions:

Do you know any good cover versions?
Are there any songs in English which have been covered by bands from your country?
Is the cover version sometimes better than the original?
Which do you think is the most covered song of all time? (Answer: 'Yesterday' by The Beatles)

2 Select and locate the original video and lyrics of a well-known song. Elicit any information the learners may know about the song (e.g. date, singer, musical style). Play the video. If it's an old song and the video is a straight performance, make sure you focus on its message, working closely with the lyrics. Learners make notes under these headings: Meaning, Genre, Style, Mood.

3 Show learners a different video version of the song. Learners compare the two versions in pairs or groups, answering these questions about the second music video:

How is the song interpreted differently?
How would you describe the change in style?
Does the video change the meaning of the song? How?
How does the narrative contribute to conveying the song's meaning?
Which one do you prefer: the original or the cover? Why?

4 Get feedback from learners. Can the class reach a consensus on the best video? Show some comments from YouTube if you need to influence the decision one way or another.

5 Learners search for other video versions of the song online and bring them into the next class. What kinds of versions are they? Professional, amateur, contemporary, a spoof? Which do they feel are the best performances? Which ones enhance the original song?

Example

'I Will Survive'

Link to original version by Gloria Gaynor (1978): youtu.be/ZBR2G-il3-I

The original video is a straight performance by Gaynor with a dancer.

Meaning: *The narrator finds personal strength after a painful break-up. She is better off without her man.*
Genre: *Disco. It has become a karaoke classic and is considered one of the greatest dance songs of all time.*
Style: *flamboyant and energetic*
Mood: *uplifting and emotionally empowering, very positive*

Link to cover version by Cake (1996): vimeo.com/32568726

How is the song interpreted differently?
It is a very simple version with guitar and vocal. It's sung by a man, not a woman. There is a guitar solo which makes it sound like a typical rock song.

How would you describe the change in style?
It is much slower and sounds sadder because there is little expression in the man's voice.

How does the video change the meaning of the song?
The video seems to have nothing to do with the topic of the song. The lead singer is a parking control officer who is putting tickets on cars. He works through the day and night. In the end, he leaves the parking lot and goes home.

How does the narrative contribute to conveying the song's meaning?
It tells the sad story of a man doing a boring job in a normal town. It almost represents the opposite to the original version. We see the other members of the band playing the song in different locations, which emphasizes its normality.

YouTube comments: You are likely to find many in favour of and against Cake's version, such as:

This is work of a pure genius. It takes a really dramatic song and transforms it into something so humdrum and everyday ;-)
They've destroyed it. The original is a hundred times better. I really like Cake but they didn't need to do this!
The original is the best. Nobody can touch it. But Cake have done it in their style and made it their own which can't be bad.

Note
A simple online search such as 'Lady Gaga covers' will find any number of different versions of her songs, from Japanese folk to amateur guitarists in their bedrooms. There are a number of well-known YouTube performers who do several cover versions. Try searching for 'best YouTube covers'.

Follow-up
For a bit of fun, check out the worst YouTube cover versions or the best spoofs of famous songs. *Rolling Stone* magazine recently chose their top ten 'worst cover songs of all time', some of which you can see the videos of (rol.st/1caeQaS).

4.4 Two songs, one video

Outline	Learners watch a mash-up (a video clip featuring two or more different songs).
Primary focus	Stimulus: imagining a video mash-up of two songs
Secondary focus	Language focus: analysis of song lyrics; language of description
Time	20–30 minutes (depending on the number of mash-ups you have)
Level	Intermediate and above
Preparation	You will need a mash-up video of two or more songs and the lyrics of the two songs. If doing mash-ups for the first time with learners who are not familiar with the concept, choose a mash-up that mixes only two songs. Music video mash-ups can be accessed on many sites including Mashup Charts (mashup-charts.com) and youtube.com/user/MashedTV

Procedure

1   Introduce the concept of a mash-up to learners if they are not aware of it. It is easier to start with a mash-up of two songs. Play the audio only from your selected mash-up video. Explain or elicit which two songs have been combined in the mash-up.

2   Play the audio again. Make sure learners are aware when one song begins and the other ends. Is there a moment when both songs are playing at the same time?

3   Ask learners to discuss why the songs have been connected. Is there a link with regard to the (1) lyrics/meaning, (2) rhythm, (3) melody, (4) style of singing? Or are the songs seemingly unrelated?

4   In pairs or groups, learners imagine a storyboard for each of the two music videos. Do they tell a story or are they abstract? What images could connect the two videos? Give them plenty of time to invent their mash-up images.

5   Play the mash-up video, pausing where necessary to allow learners to make notes describing what they see in one of the music videos, and then in the other.

6   In pairs or groups, learners compare their answers to the questions in Steps 3–5.

7   Get feedback from the class about the mash-up. What surprised or impressed them about it?

8   Finally, ask students to decide which two songs they would combine in a mash-up, and why.

Note

Mash-ups of this kind are the perfect example of today's 'remix culture'. Amateurs create new hybrids by combining different media in this way. Very often, mash-up makers combine tracks that are in the same key or have a similar rhythm. Music mash-ups are powerful because they allow us to hear new connections between tracks that listeners may not previously have believed could be connected.

Variation

There are a number of singers on YouTube who blend two different songs at the same time. The videos are often nothing other than a straight performance, but the lyrics are interesting to analyse together because there is often a thematic link. A nice task is to listen to one of these double songs and identify the lyrics of each as they are performed. Learners then analyse their differences and similarities in terms of content, genre, etc. See, for example, Sam Tsui's blended cover of 'Payphone' by Maroon 5 and 'Telephone' by Lady Gaga: youtu.be/ndOoX9c5zbA

4.5 Mash-up madness

Outline	Learners watch a music video mash-up created from different media.
Primary focus	Language focus: piecing together lyrics from a music video mash-up
Secondary focus	Resource: identifying different scenes in a music video mash-up
Time	20–30 minutes
Level	Intermediate and above
Preparation	You will need a music video mash-up of a single song. The Lionel Richie song 'Hello' is used in the example on page 92. Keep an eye out online for new mash-up creations, for example the interactive mash-up of Bob Dylan's 'Like a Rolling Stone', which the viewer can control: video.bobdylan.com/desktop

Procedure

1   Introduce the concept of a synchronized music video mash-up to the learners. It combines various clips of different people singing or saying the lyrics of a single song. Explain that the learners are going to watch a mash-up clip.
2   Tell the learners the name of the song and the original artist. Elicit or explain something about the song. What genre is it? When was it released?
3   Play the mash-up video of the song. Learners count the number of different scenes.
4   Play the clip again. In pairs or groups, learners write down any films and/or actors they recognize in the mash-up.
5   Play the video a third time. In pairs or groups, learners write down the lyrics to the song. Get feedback and make sure they are correct.
6   Learners then practise singing the song along with the video. You should orchestrate this so the first learner sings the first word or phrase on cue, the second learner the second one, and so on.

Note

There are different kinds of mash-ups. There are those in which the lyrics of a song are represented by chunks of dialogue taken from other genres (as in the 'Hello' example on page 92, where the lyrics are recreated using clips from Hollywood films). And there are those in which the song is merely a soundtrack to a collage of film clips. Finally, some mash-ups consist of people miming to the original song (as in the Bob Dylan example given in 'Preparation' above). Any type would be suitable for this activity.

Example

'Hello'

Link: vimeo.com/35055590#

Genre

Love song, originally sung by Lionel Richie in 1984

Number of extracts

43 separate clips from 37 different Hollywood films

Film clips included

Too many to list here, but the mash-up begins with clips from *E.T.*, *Bride of Frankenstein* and *Braveheart*. It also includes actors such as George Clooney and Sean Connery.

Follow-up

Learners compare the mashed-up video clip with the original video created for the song. The original video for 'Hello' is a mini drama in which Lionel Richie plays a music teacher who falls in love with a blind student.

Note

Thanks to Steve Muir for attracting my attention to the 'Hello' mash-up.

4.6 Change the soundtrack

Outline	Learners watch a video sequence without any dialogue and change the musical soundtrack to repurpose the video.
Primary focus	Skills practice: describing how to transform a video by altering the audio that accompanies the images; writing on-screen text to accompany the music
Secondary focus	Stimulus: synchronizing music and written word with images
Time	30–60 minutes
Level	Upper intermediate and above
Preparation	You will need a 'silent' video clip (2–5 minutes long). 'Silent' means there must be no dialogue, but it does not matter if there is a soundtrack. The clip should be flexible enough to be transformed into a number of different genres. Many 'silent' films are quite abstract in nature and therefore lend themselves well to this kind of task. *Note*: Part of this activity is done by the learners at home.

Procedure

1 Play your selected 'silent' video clip. If it has a soundtrack, make sure learners can't hear it at this stage. Elicit from learners different genres / purposes that the video could be used for. For example, a video of a car driven in the countryside could be a (1) car advert, (2) tourism promo for a particular country, or (3) a scene from a romantic comedy. Explain that soundtracks can reveal and enhance the genre / purpose of the video.

2 In pairs or small groups, learners select a genre for the clip, choosing from the suggestions in Step 1 or creating a new genre of their own. Learners then think of a music style that would combine well with their chosen genre and whether they will use one piece of music all the way through or change it according to the scenes shown. They can also add sounds or sound effects.

3 Learners then discuss whether they want to include any on-screen text to combine with the music. If so, when should it appear – throughout or just at the end (e.g. as an advert slogan)? They decide which group member will source the music, and arrange how to bring it to class the next day.

4 The learners bring their chosen music to the next lesson in a format which can be played in class. Play the 'silent' video to the whole class, with the learners taking it in turns to put on their soundtracks. Each group should explain how they have repurposed the video, freeze-framing to add descriptions where necessary. Provide a framework for the description similar to this:

The music we've chosen is … It turns the film into a …
At the moment, we see X. We also hear X …
When X happens, this text appears on the screen …

5 Learners listen to each group's soundtrack ideas and discuss which ones they like the best. Are there any differences or similarities between the main ideas described by the class?

Variation

If learners know how to add / change the music of a video and / or add text to the screen using Windows Movie Maker or Apple iMovie, then make the video available to them so that they can do this at home.

4.7 Videoke

Outline	Learners sing a song while watching a video and reading lyrics.
Primary focus	Skills practice: mimicking intonation and pronunciation whilst reading lyrics
Secondary focus	Language focus: comprehension and analysis of song lyrics
Time	15–30 minutes (depending on the number of songs chosen)
Level	Elementary and above
Preparation	Find a music video for a well-known song which would motivate learners. It is essential that the song lyrics are on-screen and the video should ideally show the original singer performing the song. The best videos to use are karaoke-style clips, in which the backing music is audible and the lyrics illuminate to facilitate singing in time with the music. See the Karaoke Channel (thekaraokechannel.com) or search for karaoke videos on YouTube.

Procedure

1 Prepare the learners for the music video by presenting them with the song lyrics beforehand. There are number of things you can do before watching the video, depending on whether the song is known to the class or not. If it's a very well-known song, you could either: a) present the lyrics with some errors and get learners to correct them (e.g. you could present 'It's raining men' as 'Israeli men', or 'Yesterday' could be 'Yes, Today'); or b) present the lyrics with missing words or extra words. Also elicit or provide any other background information about the song and/or the performers.

2 Once the correct version and the meaning of the lyrics is established, play the start of the music video and model a performance yourself, singing the first verse of the song. If you do this, learners are likely to feel less embarrassed about singing in class. You can also get learners to sing in pairs to reduce any possible awkwardness. *Note*: Most adult learners will have sung karaoke at some point in their lives, but explain the basic principle if necessary so that learners know when it is their cue to sing.

3 Play the whole music video. Ask learners to pay attention to the way the song is sung, to the intonation and emphasis that is placed on particular lyrics, as well as to the melody which they will need to replicate.

4 Before the singing begins, establish with the learners the lyrics which each person or pair will sing. The easiest thing to do is to go around the class left to right. Tell learners to recall the original performance and imitate the singers where possible.

5 Begin the karaoke performance. Encourage learners to pay attention to the cues in the subtitles and to imitate the original performance as best they can.

6 Do another complete performance with different learners taking different lines to sing. On this occasion, and depending on how much fun your class is having with this, learners can imitate the gestures, movements and facial expressions of the singers as well. Who is/are the best imitator(s) in the group?

7 If possible, record a performance of the song. Learners will find this motivating and put in their best performance. Allow the class to play it back later to check lyrics, melody and timing.

Note

There are auto-tune programs such as the Songify app (smule.com/songify/index) for Android and Apple smartphones which will transform speech into music. Songify is used by the Gregory Brothers, creators of the *Auto-Tune the News* series on YouTube, and other viral videos including *Bed Intruder Song*, *Can't Hug Every Cat*, *Double Rainbow* and *Winning!*. Learners can make their own videos in this way. Show them *Can't Hug Every Cat* as an example: youtu.be/sP4NMoJcFd4

Variation 1

Familiar video, new lyrics: Learners watch a video with the sound off and imagine the lyrics. They create their own lyrics and then sing along with the video. Finally, they watch with the sound on and check their version against the original. It's a good idea to choose songs with quite simple, clear lyrics for this task because learners may be able to lip read / lip sync to an extent.

Variation 2

Storyboarding the lyrics: Learners make drawings or find images to illustrate particular song lyrics. They record the images with relevant lyrics beneath them using a software package such as Windows Movie Maker. Play the students' films and the class can sing along in sync. This variation is suitable for young or basic-level learners, using songs that are short and not too complex.

Variation 3

Literal versions: Version A: Learners watch a well-known music video in which people are doing clear actions – driving, crying, running, etc. They write lyrics describing exactly what people are doing in the video, and then sing them karaoke style. These are known as 'literal versions' and many are available on YouTube and other sites. See, for example, the literal version of A-ha's 'Take On Me': youtu.be/8HE9OQ4FnkQ (13 million views in 2013). See also this 'literal version' playlist: youtube. com/playlist?list=PL69BD39AC358DB2FF

Version B: Learners watch an existing 'literal version' video but without sound. They write literal lyrics of their own and then compare with the existing 'literal version'. (Thanks to Lucy Norris for first drawing my attention to this idea.)

4.8 Performance!

Outline	Learners analyse a performance of a song to see how the text is transformed when performed.
Primary focus	Resource: analysing the performance of a written text
Secondary focus	Skills practice: annotating a text for intonation, emphasis, etc.
Time	30–60 minutes
Level	Intermediate and above (depending on the performance chosen)
Preparation	You will need a video clip showing the performance of a poem, anecdote or song. If not a song, there should be some musical quality to the performance. For example, it could be a rap or a lyrical rendition of a poem (e.g. the verse of Guyanese poet John Agard). Ideally, the text should tell a recognizable story. The example on page 97 uses a video by beatbox artist Shlomo (vimeo.com/70404609).

Procedure

1   Before showing your selected video, present learners with the text of the poem / anecdote / song being performed. Clarify any unknown language and, if necessary, ask learners to summarize it to check understanding.

2   Learners prepare to read the text out loud and think where they would insert the following features:

Emphasis (e.g. inserting italics or exclamation marks)
Dramatic pauses
Changes in rhythm – from fast to slow delivery
Changes in volume – from quiet to loud

Monitor and provide feedback where necessary.

3   A few pairs of students read out the text in class in their chosen style. Discuss as a class the differences between the various learner performances. Learners should justify why they performed it one way or another based on their choices in Step 2.

4   Play the video performance of your selected song / anecdote / poem and ask learners to analyse how the performance has transformed the text. They should make notes under any or all of these headings:

Body language / movement / gesture
Instrumentation / musical arrangement / style
Vocal range / virtuosity / delivery
Pace / rhythm

5   Finish by asking learners the following questions:

In your opinion, does the performance enhance the written word? If so, how?
What is the difference between the actual performance and how you had imagined it?
Would you like it performed in a different way? How?

Variation

If you have access to different performances of the same song, play them back-to-back and ask the learners to reflect on the differences between them with reference to the headings in Step 4. Some online media feature collated videos of cover versions of the same songs, for example: bit.ly/19YDeyq

Example

Belly Dancer by Shlomo

Link: vimeo.com/70404609

This video is a perfect example of how the performance changes and enhances the written word out of all proportion. Very little in the printed lyrics would prepare you for what is happens in the video. For this reason, these are only sample answers below. Learners may come up with different ones and reach other conclusions.

Body language / movement / gesture
A dynamic and happy performer … smiling and jumping around … we are fascinated by what he can do with his hands and mouth

Instrumentation / musical arrangement / style
Beatboxing … no instruments are used, just the performer's voice and a recorded music loop … he can be a drum, a cymbal, a metronome, etc.

Vocal range / virtuosity / delivery
Not always clear which sounds are produced by him 'live' and which are being repeated on the recorded music loop … varied vocal range

Pace / rhythm
Great changes of rhythm … the pace builds up as the song progresses … it ends very quietly on a note of reflection

---

97

5 Video and topic

These days, many coursebooks and syllabi are topic-based. A video on a topic you are focusing on in class, especially one which concerns an issue of contemporary interest, can clearly be a great way to enhance a lesson. In contrast to most of the other activities in this book, the activities in this chapter are based on specific topic-related videos, all of which are available on the Cambridge University Press ELT YouTube channel (bit.ly/CUPDigitalVideo). However, there are tips for working with clips of a similar type below and extension tasks about dealing with these topics in general.

Although each video focuses on a particular umbrella topic, the video styles here vary enormously. The video in Activity 5.2: *Water* is entirely image-based with no script as such and could be used with basic levels, while the video in Activity 5.5: *Memory* is a visual representation of a complex text and is suitable for higher levels. As with any video, we recommend that teachers view each clip in this chapter before showing it to students to ensure that the content is suitable for particular learners.

Angles

Firstly, when selecting topic-based video material, it is important to choose a universal topic which you imagine will be relevant to learners' lives. The clip should somehow explore an interesting or original angle on this familiar topic. For example, if the topic is sport, then finding a video based on a football team which didn't have a pitch to play on because they lived on a floating village (Activity 5.3: *Sport*) could prove a quirky and surprising angle. In the case of the video in Activity 5.2: *Water*, the topic is introduced by explaining the process behind the creation of an ingenious water-saving device. Bear in mind that these videos are merely examples of clips that you could find linked to these topics or any others. Hopefully, you will be inspired by these videos to find ones relevant to your context – for example, the story of a local sports team or a video that explains the working process of another invention that is of local significance. Likewise, the topic of memory (Activity 5.5) is introduced here via a poem. Using this activity as a model, you could seek out a visual poem based on a different topic of interest.

Characteristics

Another way to understand the potential of a topic-based video sequence is to break it down into its distinct characteristics. In other words, what stands out about this particular clip? What makes it special or worth watching? In the case of Activity 5.2: *Water*, flashing the key words up on screen is a key device to capture our attention. This allows for easy comprehension of how the device works and provides the springboard for the task, in which learners hypothesize about how these words will combine to create the invention. You could find another video which features lexical items flashed up in this way and use the words as a way in to exploiting the clip. In addition to text, the

style of filming is also a key characteristic for some of the videos, for example the 'tilt-shift'*
technique in Activity 5.7: *Culture*.

Similarly, in the video for Activity 5.4: *Daily life*, the use of sound to trigger topical associations
is a clear feature that is exploited in the activity procedure to engage learners' interest. You could
find a video which has an intriguing soundtrack or sound effects and exploit it in a similar way
(see Chapter 4 for more ideas involving sound and music).

Genres

In Activity 5.5: *Memory*, the video itself represents an entirely new genre – what's known as a 'visual
poem'. The visual representation enhances understanding of what would be an otherwise difficult text
for learners to unpack. Meanwhile, the video in Activity 5.6: *Humour* represents a person's life and
experiences collapsed into a crazy two-minute sequence. Apart from all of this action taking place on
a bicycle, the frenetic pace in which this video is edited is typical of the fast-moving clips so commonly
found on YouTube and other sites. Likewise, the tilt-shift filming style and time-lapse technique used
in the creation of the video in Activity 5.7: *Culture* should both appeal to and intrigue learners. As
such, it offers an unusual perspective on a country's culture.

Look out for examples of these new video genres. The novelty of the clip will help engage learners
with the topic and dictate the task procedure.

Aims / activity procedures

Once you have found a topic-based video (which possesses any of the above features), you need to
focus on the main teaching aim. The aims will govern the activity procedure that you adopt to exploit
the video. Here is a list of the main teaching aims around which the video tasks in this chapter are
based:

1 Learners create their own topic-related video content (5.1) or storyboard their own video (5.7)
   based on the material provided.
2 Learners predict the video content from topical clues (5.2 and 5.3).
3 Learners debate a topic before and after watching a video (5.3 and 5.7).
4 Learners compare their own experience with that represented in a video (5.3 and 5.5).
5 Learners analyse in detail the language used in a video script (5.5).
6 Learners cast a critical eye on the treatment of a topic (e.g. cultural features / stereotypes) seen in a
   video (5.7).
7 Learners uncover more information from multiple viewings of a video (e.g. ordering images,
   unpacking script, etc.) (5.7).
8 Learners seek out their own (in this case humorous) videos after seeing an example in class (5.6).
9 Learners summarize the video into animated stills of a graphic novel (5.1).

* Tilt-shift photography is the use of camera movements and focus to make life-sized locations or subjects look like
  miniature scenes or models.

5.1 Love

Outline	Learners turn a love story cartoon into a graphic novel.
Primary focus	Resource: using video and written text to create a graphic novel with short captions
Secondary focus	Skills practice: reconstructing and retelling a story; writing captions
Time	30–60 minutes
Level	Pre-intermediate and above (Upper intermediate and above for the follow-up debate)
Preparation	You will need the video clip *Estória do gato e da lua*, which is available on the Cambridge University Press ELT YouTube channel (bit.ly/CUPDigitalVideo).

Procedure

1 Show learners the transcript of *Estória do gato e da lua* on page 103, but don't tell them the title at this stage. Ask them to underline parts of the poem which:

   a are written in present time.
   b are written in past time.
   c are written in future time.
   d talk about waiting.
   e talk about following.
   f talk about change.
   g include images of places (e.g. ocean, roof).
   h include images of people (e.g. prisoner).

2 Get feedback from the whole class. Without looking at the transcript, learners now work in pairs or small groups to note down as many images as they can recall from it.

3 Before learners watch the video, ask them to prepare some questions that they would like answered. For example:

Why is 'she' always staring at the narrator?
Why is it so difficult to find her?
Will the narrator ever succeed?

4 Play the video once without pausing, and then ask the following questions:

How many of your questions from Step 3 were answered?
What is the poem's big surprise? (The clip is a cartoon in which 'she' is the moon and the narrator is a cat.)
How does the way the poem is read change your perception of it?
What does the final image suggest about the outcome of the love story?
How does the cartoonist use the motif of the moon throughout the poem?

5 Play the video once again. Ask learners to take note of any images that they found particularly memorable (e.g. cat running over the rooftops). They can then compare these images with those that they had thought of before watching the video.

6 Finally, learners work in groups to select six to eight video frames to prepare a graphic novel. To do this, they should read the poem carefully and think of an image that best accompanies a certain section of it. (See a selection of sample images on page 104.) It's a good idea for learners to take screenshots of the images, which may be more easily done at home and brought to class the next day. They then write a short caption for each image.

7 When each group has assembled the frames for their graphic novel, they can project them in class. They can retell the story in their own words and recite an abridged version of the poem from memory.

Follow-up

Estória do gato e da lua has been very popular on YouTube and other video-sharing platforms. Ask learners to look at a selection of viewers' comments and discuss the reasons for its popularity. You could ask the following questions as prompts:

What does it say about the topic of love that other stories don't?
What typical love story ingredients does it have?
What makes this love story special: the format, the narration of the poem, the story itself – or a combination of all three?

Estória do gato e da lua

In the beginning there was total darkness
The silent immensity of the night
Then she came and everything changed
It's been a long time since I stopped looking for her
Now everything is quieter
I learned that it's better to wait
She'll come when she can or when she wants to

I know one day she'll come to me
Otherwise why would she spend all those hours, all those nights just staring at me?

Nothing else matters
I'll wait

But it wasn't always like that
When I met her my whole life changed
I started following her
Sailed the seas
I crossed the oceans
For her I found myself drifting
I did everything to find her
And when I thought I was close, I was still very far

I felt lost not knowing what to do
In the middle of all that sea
The boat was shrinking
And the world getting smaller and smaller from all that passion

Then I changed my life
I found a steady place
And comfortably settled
I thought my proposal was irrefutable
But once again she left me
Desperate, slave of that desire
I ran after her
Jumping from roof to roof
Prisoner of that attraction
Which was slowly leaving me lonelier

And time went by…
Now I don't run anymore
I wait
Nothing else matters
I wait

Estória do gato e da lua

Sample video frames and captions

1 Waiting patiently

2 Being far away

3 Drifting at a distance

4 Getting angry

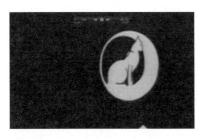

5 Chasing over rooftops

6 Waiting again

7 Finding my love / my place

From *Language Learning with Digital Video* © Cambridge University Press 2015 PHOTOCOPIABLE

5.2 Water

Outline	Learners analyse a campaign advert about saving water.
Primary focus	Stimulus: discussing innovations and inventions
Secondary focus	Skills practice / Language focus: giving instructions; vocabulary: elements used in the invention; sequencers
Time	30–60 minutes
Level	Pre-intermediate and above
Preparation	You will need the video clip *It's in Your Hands*, which is available on the Cambridge University Press ELT YouTube channel (bit.ly/CUPDigitalVideo).

Procedure

1 Elicit from learners some methods for cleaning water in areas where it is not freely available. Suggestions may include boiling, purification tablets or filters. You could tell them about the 'Lifestraw', which is a filter in the shape of a straw that cleans water as people drink it (see wikipedia.org/wiki/LifeStraw).

2 Introduce the concept of a 'Tippy Tap' (tippytap.org) – a simply made invention that allows people to wash their hands with soap and water in areas where clean running water is not available. Tell learners they are going to watch a video about the invention.

3 Introduce the different elements of the invention by drawing them on the board or showing images of the objects:
soap, matches, candle, string, water container, tools, nail, gravel, y-shaped stick, short stick.
You could take screenshots of these images from the video and project them for greater impact.

4 Distribute or project the following gapped text and ask learners to complete it with the nouns provided.

Tippy Tap

soap, matches, candle, string, water container, ~~tools~~, nail, gravel, y-shaped stick, short stick

First, you dig two holes in the ground with some **tools** and you place a long (1) _____
in each hole, about a metre apart. These form the basic structure of the Tippy Tap. Second, you take
some (2) _____ and a (3) _____ to burn a small hole in the plastic
(4) _____. After that, you stick a (5) _____ in the soap to make a hole
in it, and then put a piece of (6) _____ through it. Then, you place some loose
(7) _____ on the ground. Next, you place a (8) _____ across the two
Y-shaped sticks to make the top of the Tippy Tap. You tie the water container to the Tippy Tap structure
and fill it with water. Finally, you tie on the bar of (9) _____. To make the invention
work, you use another short stick and piece of string as a lever. You can now use the Tippy Tap to wash
your hands easily with soap and water.

From *Language Learning with Digital Video* © Cambridge University Press 2015   PHOTOCOPIABLE

---

5 Get feedback from the class, but do not give correct answers at this stage. Focus attention on the sequencers: *first, second, after that, then, next, finally.*
6 Ask learners to make a few visual predictions about the video. For example, ask them to think about who is building the invention and where. What colour is the water container and how much water can it hold?
7 Play the whole video and ask learners to check their answers to the gapfill task in Step 4. (Answers: 1 *y-shaped stick*, 2 *matches*, 3 *candle*, 4 *water container*, 5 *nail*, 6 *string*, 7 *gravel*, 8 *short stick*, 9 *soap*.) They can also check their visual predictions from Step 6.
8 Get final feedback from learners about the video. Is there anything that surprised them about it? Do they think it is an effective campaign clip? Why? Why not?

Figure 5.1: Still image from *It's in Your Hands*

Follow-up
You could show the class other videos connected to water, or ask learners to find some of their own to share. Some suggestions are:
GOOD: Water (youtu.be/HW5eBfZhE4M)
The Story of Bottled Water (youtu.be/Se12y9hSOMo)
EXPO Water city (vimeo.com/15940064).

Note
This video activity uses the tactic of delaying the showing of the clip until the last moment. Students first work closely with vocabulary to try and work out how the invention is constructed, so they are very familiar with the concept before seeing it. They should then be motivated to see how the real thing operates and the video becomes a reward for all their language work.

Variation
The same task could be done with any invention, particularly if its construction / operation is relatively easy to explain.

5.3 Sport

Outline	Learners analyse a short film about a junior Thai football team.
Primary focus	Stimulus: discussing the universal topic of football
Secondary focus	Skills practice / Language focus: reading subtitles; language of giving opinions; ways of being emphatic
Time	30–60 minutes
Level	Upper intermediate and above
Preparation	You will need the *Panyee FC* video which is available on the Cambridge University Press ELT YouTube channel (bit.ly/CUPDigitalVideo).

Procedure

1 Present the learners with these statements about football. Individually, learners decide whether they agree or disagree with them. They then add two or three statements of their own.

Football ...

... is the most popular sport in my country.
... breaks through barriers and brings people together.
... is all about money nowadays.
... is not about winning but taking part.
... has as many female fans as male fans.
... is a form of escape.

... _____

... _____

... _____

From *Language Learning with Digital Video* © Cambridge University Press 2015   PHOTOCOPIABLE

---

2 Learners share their opinions with classmates. Introduce and model some key structures for giving opinions to help them. For example:

I totally agree with ...　　　　*That's so true.*
That's absolutely right.　　　*I'm not sure about this.*
I don't agree with this at all.　*That's completely wrong!*

3 Show learners a still image from the *Panyee FC* video, like the one in Figure 5.2 on page 108. Ask the learners:

Where do you think this place is?
What is strange about the football pitch?
Who is going to play on it?
Do you think the film will be about:
a *a specific football team?*
b *how to play football surrounded by water?*
c *the role of football in society?*

Figure 5.2: Still image from *Panyee FC*

4 Play the video and ask learners to check their answers to the questions in Step 3.
5 Learners watch the film again and answer these questions:

What is surprising about the film?
What element of the film most impressed you: the story, the acting, the direction or the element of surprise?
What is the overall message of the film?

6 Learners now revisit the football statements in Step 1. Which statements are most relevant to the film? Have learners changed their opinions about any of the statements, having watched the video?
7 Tell learners that the film was made as an advertisement for TMB, one of the largest banks in Thailand. Ask learners the following questions to finish the lesson:

Does the involvement of the bank change your opinion about the film?
Why do you think a bank would make a film about a football team?
What message might they be transmitting with this film?

Note
TMB (the Thai bank that commissioned the advert) decided to tell the story of Panyee FC, a football team from a small fishing village in southern Thailand. They felt the story would help launch their new brand philosophy: *Make the Difference*. The film launched on YouTube and quickly became very popular. Half a million separate web pages published the film and eventually the film reached over 1.3 billion people worldwide. The players from Panyee quickly became one of the most popular football teams on the planet.

Follow-up
Learners find any interesting videos on YouTube or Vimeo on the subject of football. For example, what fan-made films are available? How have the fans made/edited them? What soundtracks have they added, etc.?

Variation

For an advanced class you could present learners with the following text in Step 1 and ask them to give their opinions about it. The learners could then seek out video material that exemplifies the points made in the text.

The Ball Is Round: A Global History of Football

David Goldblatt (2006)

Is there any cultural practice more global than football? [...] No single world religion can match its geographical scope. [...] The use of English and the vocabularies of science and mathematics must run football close for universality but they remain the lingua franca of the world's elite, not of its masses. McDonalds, MTV? Only the most anodyne products of America's cultural industries can claim to reach as wide as football, and then only for a fleeting moment in those parts of the world that can afford them. [...] Football is available to anyone who can make a rag ball and find another pair of feet to pass to. Football has not merely been consumed by the world's societies, it has been embraced, embedded and then transformed by them.

From *Language Learning with Digital Video* © Cambridge University Press 2015   PHOTOCOPIABLE

5.4 Daily life

Outline	Learners watch a film about routines.
Primary focus	Stimulus: discussing daily life in India
Secondary focus	Skills practice / Language focus: writing a diary entry; present simple for routines; language of comparison
Time	30–60 minutes
Level	Pre-intermediate and above
Preparation	You will need the video clip *Amar (all great achievements require time)* which is available on the Cambridge University Press ELT YouTube channel (bit.ly/CUPDigitalVideo).

Procedure

1 Ask learners to read the following video blurb. Explain any unknown vocabulary, for example *breadwinner*.

Amar (all great achievements require time)

Amar is 14 and top of his class. Someday he'd like to be a professional cricketer, but for now he's the family's main breadwinner, working two jobs six and a half days a week on top of attending school in the afternoons. This short observational documentary is a simple journey with Amar through his daily life.

From *Language Learning with Digital Video* © Cambridge University Press 2015   PHOTOCOPIABLE

---

2 Explain that learners are going to watch a film about Amar's daily life in Jamshedpur, a fast-growing industrial city in eastern India, known as 'Steel City'. Before doing so, present the learners with these questions for discussion in pairs or small groups:

When you were 14, what was your daily life like? What was your routine?
What two jobs do you think Amar does?
What do you think he studies at school?
How do you imagine that Amar gets around the city?
The film is described as an 'observational documentary'. What do you think this means? What do you imagine the film will be like?

3 Play the first minute of the video (until the rooster crows) but do not allow learners to see the screen yet. They are just listening to the soundtrack at this point. Ask the learners to write down any sounds that they hear (sample answers: *crickets chirping, tap running, brushing of teeth, putting clothes on, a bicycle, some murmuring of people saying goodbye*).

4 Using their notes, learners visualize images that might appear in the video and describe these to classmates. What do the people, scenery and buildings look like? What objects can be seen? What is the weather like?

5 Play the first minute of the video again, this time with the screen in view. Learners compare their visualizations with the images in the video. What are the similarities and differences?

6 Now play the whole video. Ask learners to check their answers to the questions in Step 2.

7 Get feedback from the class. Then present the learners with the following statements about the story. Ask learners to decide whether they are true or false. If false, they should correct them.

a Amar's mother wakes up at the same time as him.
b Amar delivers the newspapers to each person's door.
c He doesn't have time to read the newspaper.
d He studies.
e He takes a shower at 2pm.
f He eats lunch with his family.
g He polishes his shoes to go to school.
h He goes to an all-boys school.
i He works in an electrical shop in the afternoon.
j He sleeps about seven hours a night.

Answers:
a True
b False (He throws the papers into people's apartments.)
c False (He reads the paper at 6am.)
d True
e False (He has a wash at 1pm.)
f True
g True
h False (He goes to a mixed school.)
i True
j False (He wakes up at 3.58am and goes to bed at about 10.30pm, so he only sleeps about five and a half hours.)

Follow-up

Learners write a short diary of Amar's day. They can find out more about the relationship between Amar and the film director from the *Calcutta Telegraph* (bit.ly/1ktfFEN).

Note

Thanks to Kieran Donaghy for pointing me in the direction of this film on his Film English site (film-english.com).

5.5 Memory

Outline	Learners watch a visual poem about memory loss.
Primary focus	Stimulus: discussing memory; comparing learners' experience with that of the poet
Secondary focus	Skills practice/Language focus: detailed understanding of lexis used in poem; memorizing visual information
Time	30–60 minutes
Level	Upper Intermediate/Advanced
Preparation	You will need the video clip *Forgetfulness*, which is available on the Cambridge University Press ELT YouTube channel (bit.ly/CUPDigitalVideo). You will also need a transcript of the poem for Step 4 (see poemhunter.com/poem/forgetfulness).

Procedure

1 Learners think of a poem that they know well and like. Ask them what they remember about it and why they like it. How do they think this poem could be made more accessible for the 'digital generation'?

2 Play the video of the visual poem *Forgetfulness*. Ask learners to number images A–H below in the order they see them.

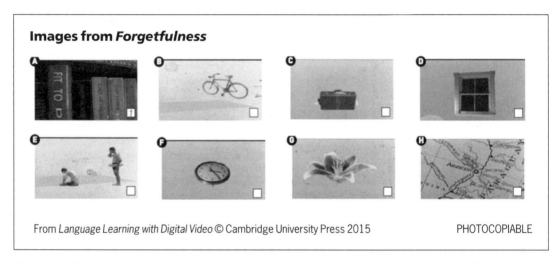

Images from *Forgetfulness*

From *Language Learning with Digital Video* © Cambridge University Press 2015   PHOTOCOPIABLE

3 Play the video again and ask learners to list the things that the poet has forgotten in relation to images A–H above. (For example, Image A [books on shelves] relates to forgotten details about a novel.)

Answers: B how to ride a bike; C quadratic equation; D words of a love poem; E how to swim; F date of a battle; G name of a flower; H capital of Paraguay.

4 After showing the video a third time, distribute transcripts of the poem so learners can do these text-based tasks:

  a Find seven synonyms for *disappear* or *vanish*.
     (answers: *go, retire, kiss goodbye, pack its bag, slip away, float away, drift out of*)
  b Find six expressions related to 'remembering'.
     (answers: *harbour, memorize, on the tip of your tongue, lurk, recall, know by heart*)

5 Learners choose the best summary of the poem from these options (suggested answer: 2 or 5):

  1 Our memories are random; we remember some things and forget others.
  2 We try to remember things, but the more we do this, the harder they are to recall.
  3 We can't remember trivial things and things we learned at school.
  4 We forget everything eventually, and this is infuriating.
  5 Very important, meaningful things can be forgotten easily; everything is ephemeral.

6 Finally, learners discuss their own memories. Do they remember or forget the same kinds of things as those expressed in the poem? How would they express their forgetfulness visually?

Variation
Learners read and analyse the poem first and hypothesize about its visual representation. They watch the video and check their answers. What features of the poem were enhanced by the video version? Were there any parts of the verse that could have been represented in a better way? What changes would they make, if any?

Note
A version of this activity first appeared in *English Unlimited Advanced Self-study Pack* (Ben Goldstein and Maggie Baigent, Cambridge University Press, 2011).

5.6 Humour

Outline	Learners watch a humorous video about life on a bike.
Primary focus	Stimulus: viewing for detail
Secondary focus	Language focus: verb–noun collocations (*fry an egg*, *brush your teeth*, etc.)
Time	30 minutes
Level	Elementary and above
Preparation	You will need the video clip *The Man Who Lived On His Bike* which is available on the Cambridge University Press ELT YouTube channel (bit.ly/CUPDigitalVideo).

Procedure

1 Tell learners that they are going to a watch a humorous video called *The Man Who Lived On His Bike*. As a warmer, ask learners what they like or don't like about riding a bike.

2 Brainstorm with learners what everyday actions you could possibly do on a bike in addition to cycling (e.g. brush your teeth with one hand, answer your mobile phone, send a text). Learners think of as many actions as possible – the more ridiculous the better.

3 Play the video twice. In pairs, learners try to identify as many actions as they can. How many of them did they think of beforehand?

4 Learners then work in groups to build up their list of actions. Get feedback from the class on the funniest, strangest or most memorable actions.

5 Learners watch the video a third time to confirm their final list. Are there any actions that they missed? At the same time, ask learners to comment on any other funny elements, for example the cyclist's costumes and wigs, what he is carrying, etc.

6 Get feedback from the whole class. Finish by discussing the nature of the video's humour. Brainstorm different kinds of humour with higher-level learners (e.g. black comedy, slapstick, sarcasm, irony, etc.).

Note

The film was made by the cyclist Guillaume Blanchet. It was shot in Montreal and was compiled from 382 different days of cycling around the city. Please view the clip before showing it your learners to check that it is suitable for them, as there is some partial nudity in the earlier scenes.

Many videos on YouTube and Vimeo adopt this sudden jump-cut format for comic and dramatic effect. A well-known example is *Matt Dancing* (youtu.be/zlfKdbWwruY). In this case, the dancer stays the same, but the place where he is dancing (the backdrop) changes constantly.

Variation

Learners prepare a series of questions for the film-maker. What challenges do you think the cyclist faced in making the movie? To help answer the questions, show learners the video of how the film was made: *The Man Who Lived On His Bike / Making of* (vimeo.com/38060089).

5.7 Culture

Outline	Learners watch a video that encapsulates a country's culture.
Primary focus	Resource: analysing a video as a source of information about a culture
Secondary focus	Stimulus: discussion about cultural stereotypes and misconceptions
Time	30–60 minutes
Level	Pre-intermediate and above
Preparation	You will need the video clip *Sweet Spain,* which is available on the Cambridge University Press ELT YouTube channel (bit.ly/CUPDigitalVideo).

Procedure

1 Learners first reflect on their own culture by thinking of a few words or ideas for each of these eight headings:

Climate	*Food and drink*	*Architecture / Monuments*	*Music*
Sport	*People / Lifestyle*	*Entertainment / Pastimes*	*Landscape*

2 If you are in a monolingual context, learners can compare their notes in pairs or small groups. If not, learners use their notes to explain something about their own culture to classmates.

3 Learners now turn their attention to the cultural characteristics of Spain. What would they expect to find in a short video about this country? (e.g. sunny weather, flamenco music, olive trees, etc.). At this stage, bear in mind any stereotypes or misconceptions that may arise but don't refer to or dwell on them.

4 Play the video *Sweet Spain* (or any other short video based around a country's culture – see 'Note 2' on page 116 for another example). Learners make a note of any cultural characteristics shown in the video and compare in groups (a summary of images from the clip is given on page 116).

5 Get feedback from the whole class using the following questions as prompts:

Which characteristics coincided with your predictions?
Which concepts are new to you?
Which features did you find the most interesting or original?
Were any elements stereotypical or did they represent an outsider's view of a culture?
What is the overall feeling transmitted about Spain in the video?

6 In a monolingual class, ask learners to plan a video about their own culture. They list elements they would include under the headings in Step 1 and then create a storyboard of the different scenes they would shoot.

7 Once they have finished, encourage learners to reflect on their choices. Is their vision different from a stereotypical one? Did they include any elements which could be considered negative? What soundtrack did they choose and why?

Note 1

Sweet Spain is an example of a 'tilt-shift' film. Tilt-shift photography is the use of camera movements and focus to make life-sized locations or subjects look like miniature scenes or models. Another tilt-shift film made by the same director, Joerg Daiber, is *Beautiful Beijing* (vimeo.com/76940203). Learners can make their own tilt-shift videos using tiltshiftvideoapp.com

Note 2

So Long, My Hong Kong (vimeo.com/52948373) is another example of a homage to a particular country's culture. Such videos can be used for intercultural awareness raising, or to allow learners to reflect on their own country, its perceived image and how it is 'sold' to tourists.

Variation

In a multilingual class, ask learners to work in pairs to plan a video that compares their two cultures side-by-side (e.g. a Mexican student might show people eating tacos in the street, while a Chinese student might show people eating dim sum in a crowded restaurant).

Sweet Spain

Summary of main images

Climate	sunshine, heat, blue skies
Food and drink	N/A
Architecture/Monuments	city palaces, picturesque squares, fountains, villages with small white-painted houses
Music	soundtrack is lively, passionate, classical
Sport	rowing
People/Lifestyle	relaxed, tourists in queues to see monuments
Entertainment/Pastimes	bullfighting, boating
Landscape	mountains, ravines, dry landscape, olive groves, riverside scenes in city

---

Part 2: Video creation

Introduction

1 Digital video creation

A learner-centred, hands-on approach is at the core of the video-creation activities and projects in this chapter. Activities vary in length from short 30-minute tasks to project-based learning ideas that can remain ongoing throughout a whole term or semester. Many of these do not fit into neat categories. They are multi-modal projects designed to engage learners in the creative process. This often requires practices that embody complex contexts and procedures and encourage collaboration. Often the end result of these activities is of less importance than the process leading to it. The primary goals are *situating language through practical engagement* in the creation of digital artefacts. This is achieved through the process of guided reflection, critical thinking, performance, debate, design, creativity and other competences often referred to as '21st-century skills'. The role of the teacher becomes one of learning facilitator and project manager, rather than content deliverer and, as is typical with any form of active or project-based learning, notions of timing and control need to be flexible.

While language goals are explicitly defined, these are in no way intended to be prescriptive. Many of the activities can easily be adapted to focus on a wide variety of language points and skills development. By working through the projects and activities, learners are encouraged to identify patterns or trends, examine perspectives and alternate points of view, predict, analyse causal relationships, and create original content both *in* and *through* English.

In *Hard Times*, Charles Dickens explores the ideology of an education system that views students as empty 'vessels' needing to be filled with 'nothing but facts'. Imagination, play and creativity are aggressively discouraged as a wasteful distraction, the teacher's responsibility being to 'kill outright the robber Fancy lurking within'. Although over 160 years have passed since its writing, this, unfortunately, still sounds painfully familiar. A Google Image search using the term 'classroom' reveals that the organizational structure of the typical Victorian classroom is still very much alive and well, and, embedded in the design of these face-front learning spaces, is still the tacit notion that knowledge is transmitted from a 'sage on the stage'. Blackboards may have morphed into whiteboards, interactive screens and data projections, but it seems learners are still *sitting* and *looking* in the same direction.

The goal of learning a foreign language is complex, nuanced, socially embedded and physically embodied, yet the process of learning is so often streamlined, sequential and dissociated from everyday settings and meaningful action. Context, agency and communicative authenticity all too often become peripheral considerations and the physical limitations of classroom spaces are, at least partially, to blame.

James Gee (2004, p.39) expresses this astutely:

> Learning does not work well when learners are forced to check their bodies at the schoolroom door like guns in the old West. School learning is often about disembodied minds learning outside any context of decisions and actions. When people learn something as a cultural process their bodies are involved because cultural learning always involves having specific experiences that facilitate learning, not just memorizing words.

Dewey also highlights and critiques this epistemological 'severing' of the body and mind, viewing learning as an emergent property of engaging with the world through action, experience and goal-oriented problem solving within complex environments. You push against the world and it pushes back at you.

> In schools, those under instruction are too customarily looked upon as acquiring knowledge as theoretical spectators, minds which appropriate knowledge by direct energy of intellect. The very word pupil has almost come to mean one who is engaged not in having fruitful experiences but in absorbing knowledge directly. (Dewey, 1916, p.140)

In recent years there have been many pedagogical experiments that have attempted to reinterpret or break out of the classroom box completely, such as the 'flipped classroom' approach and MOOCs (massive open online courses). While both of these approaches use digital media to redefine and extend learning beyond the boundaries of the classroom, they are still very much content *consumption* oriented.

Gee, on the other hand, envisages a more creative, democratic and subversive application of digital media: 'Digital media again offer us an opportunity for equality, for letting everyone be producers as well as consumers. With digital media people can often bypass official institutions and oversight to produce their own media, knowledge, products, services, and texts' (2011, p.3).

The concept of meaning-making through interaction lies at the centre of the constructivist view of learning, and can be traced back much further to Dewey's philosophy of hands-on or experiential education (1916) and before. In the social constructivist view, knowledge is first constructed in a social context, before being appropriated through the individual process of assimilation and accommodation. The world becomes intelligible to us as we build and negotiate meanings through experience in conjunction with others or with cultural artefacts. Slowly, we are seeing a shift away from the acquisition and accumulation metaphor of knowledge towards a creation, participation and collaboration metaphor, in which knowledge is considered to be generated through, and fundamentally rooted in, practice. This framing of knowledge generation as an explorative, heuristic process is already common outside of formal education and is, for example, central to the design of many of the most highly engaging video games. It is often the case that learners who struggle to maintain focus in classes may, voluntarily, spend untold hours wrestling with hugely complex, technical and strategic problems when they are embedded within the interactive worlds of video games.

'Levelling up' is a key concept in the design of video games. It implies progression and the learning of new skills and abilities that will prepare you for the challenges ahead. When you have mastered one level, you move on or up to the next. Of course, I am aware that real life isn't that simple or linear and different people will have an untidy mix of experience and competence in different areas.

Nevertheless, I think the gaming roots of the term suggest a certain playfulness that should be at the heart of creative task design. Playfulness is also a healthy way of approaching the process of learning to use new technologies (and language of course!) through fearless experimentation and fun.

The different sections in Part 2: *Creation* are organized according to logistical complexity, the technological know-how required and the amount of creative, imaginative or dramatic challenge involved. As all of these things can be quite subjective, and also many of the projects have mixed components in which one aspect may be challenging and the others less so, use these levels as guides only. They are not in any way prescriptive or objective divisions. What all the creation projects and activities have in common is that they promote active learning and develop communicative competence while also helping learners to develop the skills, theory and practice they need to create, collaborate and share their own content.

2 Tech tips and advice

Green screens

Figure A: Using a green screen

Filming against green screens enables you to make the background of a video clip transparent, so that you can substitute it for anything you like in post production. This is known as 'chroma keying'. Green screens are commonly used in television newsrooms, weather reports, Hollywood movies and video games to create virtual environments, such as animated weather maps and some of the most dazzling special effects that you see in the latest blockbuster films and games.

Blue screens can also be used, and might be better suited in certain situations, such as when your subject is wearing green or there are green objects in the scene such as plants. Generally, though, green screens produce better results in the classroom, as the sensors in digital cameras are more sensitive to green light (because of something known as 'Bayer pattern filtering'). This means that you do not have to be overly concerned about lighting your scene perfectly. The unnatural shade of green used in green screens is also found quite rarely in clothing and is a long way from human skin tones on the colour spectrum.

Green screens provide an easy, effective way to integrate a human subject with other types of content in order to illustrate what is being said and provide context for the language being produced. You can blend in slides from a presentation, screenshots from a video game, holiday photos, footage shot on location or animated digital motion backgrounds. If you pay attention to a few small details, you can use them with your learners to create high-quality, professional-looking video productions that they will be proud of and want to share. And all this with very little effort or technical know-how.

Figure B: Adding the background

Types of green screen

The type of green screen you choose will depend on several factors, though first and foremost is likely to be the budget you have available. Other considerations will be the amount of space you have for filming, whether you want your screen to be permanent or portable and whether you will be filming mostly indoors or outside on location.

Paper or card

Probably the cheapest option is to buy several large sheets of fluorescent or vividly green paper and then tape them together (at the back so the tape doesn't show) to form a screen that fits the space available. Aside from being cheap, another advantage of this method is that you can quickly and easily dismantle the screen after filming if the space is needed for other things. Also, if it gets damaged, individual sections can be replaced, and if a larger screen is needed you can simply extend it by adding more sheets.

On the downside, it can be quite troublesome to have to tape and then unstick the sheets after every use if you are working in a multi-use space. This is also the least robust method as the paper or card can quickly become damaged. Moreover, if the card is the wrong hue, this may lead to poor results. The best shade of green to use is often referred to as 'chroma key green', and it is quite a vivid, almost fluorescent, colour. Certain types of paper and card may also reflect light back at the camera, which can ruin the effect. In general though, this budget approach can produce acceptable results.

Chroma key paint

Unlike normal household paints, this special type of paint is completely matte and will not cause those annoying reflections that can ruin the background transparency effect. It is an ideal option if you would like to create a permanent classroom screen. Chroma key paint can be quite expensive, but it is the most trouble-free way to get started quickly as once it has been painted, there is no taping, mounting or transporting to be done.

However, as this will be a permanent screen, if you do choose this option make sure that you select the location to paint your screen carefully, taking into consideration the lighting, room acoustics and the space you have available.

Cloth

Cloth green screens are essentially just cotton sheets. They are relatively cheap to buy and come in many different sizes. As they are commonly used in photography studios, they are also very easy to find or order online. They come ready-made in the right chroma key shade of green, and the fabric scatters light well, eliminating reflections. Many also come with a pocket along the top of the screen so that you can insert a curtain pole or rod to suspend it. Alternatively, you can pin the cloth to the wall. I prefer to insert a flat length of wood through the pocket instead of a rod so that I can rest it on top of the classroom whiteboard.

At the end of a filming session, cloth screens can simply be rolled up or folded and put away in a drawer. A drawback to this is that, over time, folds and wrinkles can develop. These can cause uneven lighting and shadows, reducing the quality of the final outcome. All the green-screen projects in this book have been carried out using cloth screens, as I have found them to be the most adaptable and convenient option for filming in a wide variety of spaces. They will need to be ironed now and again though, which can be quite awkward with larger screens. If this is a concern, a slightly more expensive foam-backed cloth might be a more manageable choice as these are virtually wrinkle-proof.

If only a small area is required to film the head and shoulders of just one person at a time, collapsible cloth screens are a good option. They are very handy as they have a built-in frame that helps to keep the material taut. They often come with a loop at the top for easy hanging and some of them are reversible, with chroma key green on one side and blue on the other.

Lighting

In order to achieve a professional effect, it is important to light your screen evenly from both sides. This will eliminate any shadows from your subject and create an even tone that makes it easier for your editing software to distinguish between the foreground and background layers. As I mentioned earlier though, green screens are quite tolerant of poor lighting and good results can be achieved without the need for special lighting equipment. Brightness is important, however, as is the avoidance of shadows. For this reason, whenever possible, I set up my screens to take advantage of side lighting from windows. If strong light is coming in from only one side, a simple trick such as using the light from a portable data projector as a counterbalance can make a big difference. It's always a good idea to try out several spots to see where you can get the best results, and to turn lights off and on to see whether they're helping or hindering your plans. Fortunately, classrooms are of necessity quite brightly lit places, and none of the projects included in this book have required any special lighting provisions.

Space

Classrooms are often quite cramped spaces and not designed with the forethought of them being transformed into film studios. Fortunately, though, setting up a green screen takes up very little space. Probably the most essential spatial consideration is to make sure that there is some distance (at least a metre) between where your subject is standing and the green screen. This is especially important if there is overhead lighting in the centre of the room, as this can cause a strongly contrasting shadow to fall on the screen. If this happens, the problem can usually be resolved quite simply by asking your subject to take a step forwards.

Software

As processing power and memory capacity have increased, extremely powerful video-editing software has moved from the desktop to the laptop and now to mobile devices such as tablets and smartphones. Prices have also plummeted to the point where these applications are often bundled for free when you buy a new computer or phone. Many of the features that not so long ago were available only to professionals with deep pockets have trickled down to become standard features of consumer software packages.

While Adobe Premiere Pro and Apple's Final Cut Pro still rule the roost at the high end of professional software, both companies offer much cheaper versions that are better suited to the non-professional. Windows Movie Maker is currently free to download and can be used for most of the creation projects in this book. However, at present it does not provide an easy way to achieve the green screen effect. Apple's iMovie and the Pinnacle Studio series are both cheap alternatives that are more than capable. At the time of writing, iMovie is free with every new Mac and iOS device. While perfectly adequate for most tasks, the mobile versions of these software packages are often deprived of the more advanced features offered by the laptop/desktop versions, so it is wise to check whether they include any special tools that you may require for a particular project before buying them.

Video can also be edited directly from within the browser without the need to instal any software at all. There are a growing number of sites that provide this service, but one of the easiest to use is YouTube's own video-editing capability, which can be found at youtube.com/editor. Online editors usually offer quite basic functionality and can be slow to work with. They are currently best suited for shorter clips that require only simple editing.

As software developers have sought to harmonize the user interfaces of their software across devices, these applications have become easier to grasp and more intuitive to use. They have also appropriated the same physical metaphors of cut, copy, paste, and drag and drop that are instantly recognizable to the vast majority of computer users. While there are many free tutorials to be found across the Web, no special training is required to learn the basic skills necessary to carry out the projects in this book.

I will not even attempt to provide a written step-by step guide to the process of editing video, as the specific functions, options, workflows and interfaces vary enough across different applications to make this impractical. In addition, as the pace of publishing cannot hope to keep up with the rate of technological change, any instructions I might provide here would certainly be outdated by the time you read them. Only last week, split screen and picture-in-picture capability was added to the mobile version of Apple's iMovie, something that had previously involved quite convoluted workarounds.

In my experience, by far the best way to learn video editing is by *editing video*. Just film something for 10 to 20 seconds, import it into whatever software you have access to (this is nearly always as easy as choosing *file* and then selecting *import*) and then just play around and have fun. Click on things, open menus, apply effects, cut your clip into pieces, change the order, make it play in slow motion, work through a tutorial, add some titles, re-dub the audio, and so on. See what you can do. Test the limits of the software and your imagination.

Hardware

Now that video editing has descended from its ivory tower and become an everyday cheap and easy-to-master activity, more and more people are shooting video on their phones. These multi-functional miracles have replaced the expensive and clunky camcorders of yesteryear and are capable of capturing high-definition video. With each generation of device, better-quality lenses and digital sensors are introduced, along with important features like optical image stabilization to counter the camera shake that such lightweight devices are prone to. In tandem, mobile video-editing software has also greatly improved. All of these things have converged and the convenience of being able to edit and share video on the fly is proving to be a powerful motivator.

That's all well and good, but for classroom use and longer projects, editing video on a tiny screen can prove to be a frustrating and meticulous process. Tablets provide a much better platform because of their more practical screen sizes, more powerful processing and increased storage capacity. Nevertheless, laptops are currently still the best option, in my opinion, as they combine portability with power and are able to run the most feature-complete versions of the editing software. For some of the video-creation activities and projects in this book, the most efficient workflow would be for the learners, when possible, to use their mobile devices for capturing the footage they need before passing the files over to their laptops or classroom computers to carry out the editing tasks.

One further piece of classroom hardware that I would highly recommend is a flexible tripod. These can be used to secure smartphones to virtually any object, as the rubberized legs can be folded around the edges of tables, grip the tops of chairs or stand upright on the most uneven surfaces. They are cheap and very portable, and special versions are available that have been specifically designed to secure smartphones of varying sizes.

Sound

It's very easy to get caught up in the visual side of video production and neglect sound quality. The vast majority of classroom video projects that you can find on the Web suffer from this, leaving behind an archive of muffled, unintelligible speech peppered with background noise. While classrooms, especially the larger ones with hard floors and empty walls, rarely provide the ideal controlled acoustic environment you might wish for, a few simple tips and equipment choices can make an enormous difference.

Many smartphones now feature dual microphones for cancelling background noise and echo and can produce surprisingly crisp sound. In smallish classrooms these are often good enough, especially if the room is carpeted and the subject being filmed is not too far away. If this is not the case, however, then you may want to use an external USB microphone that you can connect directly to a laptop.

I often use an old USB Blue Snowball mic in my classes for both podcasting and video production. They are extremely robust but sensitive condenser microphones (this particular one has survived being knocked around in my bag and classes for many years), and they have a switch on the back that enables you to choose between cardioid and omnidirectional input. The cardioid setting is ideal for recording audio in a noisy classroom, as it only records sound sources that are directly in front of the microphone, ignoring noises coming from the sides and behind the mic. The omnidirectional setting, as the name suggests, records sound from all angles. This may be handy in certain situations, such as when you wish to capture a particular soundscape, but it is of relatively little use for the purposes suggested in this book. Another tip is to use a long USB cable to connect the microphone to your laptop. This will enable you to position it much closer to the subject.

Lapel or 'lavalier' microphones are another option. These are commonly used in broadcasting as they are small and inconspicuously clip onto the speaker's shirt or jacket. As they are close to the speaker's mouth, the sound quality is usually very good and although they are usually omnidirectional, they are not powerful enough to pick up background noise.

Sharing

The completion of a video-creation project does not have to be the conclusion of the learning experience. Learners can present their work to others beyond the classroom by sharing their videos online. The idea of sharing the outcome with a public audience can enhance the authenticity of the learning experience, increase engagement and prove to be a powerful motivator for learners to produce work of a high quality. It also creates an archive of their work that can be reflected upon and integrated into a learning portfolio. Sharing the outcome of their work also provides an invaluable opportunity for receiving (and giving) feedback from (or to) others.

One important question to consider is *where* to share the videos created by the learners. There is no simple answer to this, as your choice will need to be based on the age of your learners, privacy, cultural and ethical considerations, institutional policy and the technology available to you. These will have to be aligned and balanced with the learning goals of each project or activity.

If your school or university has its own learning management system (LMS) or virtual learning environment (VLE), then this may be the ideal place to share your learners' work. As these require a login and are not public, access permissions can be limited or granted only to specific individuals or groups.

YouTube allows users to create an account and set up a video channel that can be managed to share videos only with specific individuals/groups/communities (if you link your channel to a Google+ account), with anyone who has the link (which is unlisted), or to give complete open access to a video. Just go to 'Privacy settings' and select from 'Public', 'Unlisted' or 'Private'. Vimeo also allows users to create a channel and control access to the uploaded content. Again, go to 'Privacy settings' and choose who can see your channel: 'Anyone', 'Only moderators' or 'Only moderators and people I choose'.

Both services also allow you to share your videos elsewhere by embedding them on a class blog or webpage. Alternatively, using augmented reality apps such as Aurasma and Layar, learner-generated video can be embedded in the physical environment of the school or classroom and shared.

Cloud services such as Dropbox, Skydrive and Google Drive can also be a good way to share video content with individual learners. However, storage space can quickly become an issue if the videos are shot in high resolution, as the file sizes will be large. Specific folders can be shared with a class or learners can be provided with a link to download an individual video clip.

Physical media such as thumb drives or SD cards can also be used to share videos, although this can be time-consuming and unwieldy in a classroom context.

References

Dewey, J. (1916) *Democracy and Education: An Introduction to the Philosophy of Education*, London: Macmillan.

Gee, J. P. (2004) *Situated Language and Learning: A critique of traditional schooling*, New York: Routledge.

Gee, J. P. and Hayes, E. R. (2011) *Language and Learning in the Digital Age*, New York: Routledge.

6 Straightforward video creation: Level 1

As the chapter title suggests, the following activities and projects have been grouped because of their relative simplicity to set up and use with a class. I do, however, still recommend trying out *any* task that involves creating content in advance, or at least running through the different stages.

Several of the projects covered in Level 1 focus on improving digital literacy by raising awareness of the constructed nature and generic features of popular media. For example, Activity 6.4: *Good game?* takes learners through the process of dissecting, analysing and discussing the characteristics of *good* video games, before playing one and recording a video review. Similarly, Activity 6.2: *Meme machine* guides learners to deconstruct the 'DNA' of popular viral videos into a recipe, which they then follow to create their own memes and share with the world.

Other tasks take a more personal tone, such as Activity 6.1: *Limelight*, which focuses on showcasing individual talents, interests or abilities, while also developing basic digital video-recording skills that will help to familiarize the learners with the capabilities of their own mobile devices.

Activity 6.5: *Lip service* introduces audio editing as a means of situating language (metaphorically and literally) in the context of a video clip that has become separated from its audio track. This audio track, which has been cut into Lego-like blocks and shuffled, needs to be reassembled and repositioned by the learners to match what they can see. It is then re-synchronized with the video. Aside from providing intensive listening practice, this activity helps to develop abductive reasoning, as learners combine contextual visual clues in the video with language cues in the audio. Activity 6.3: *Voice-over substitution* also involves basic audio-recording and editing skills, while drawing attention to the journalistic language of news reports. In this activity the learners' attention is drawn to the speed and intonation of a news presenter's speech, which they use as a model to record their own voice-overs.

6.1 Limelight

Outline	Learners create a video demonstrating a special talent, ability or interest they have and present it in class.
Primary focus	Describing skills, talents and personal interests (adverbs of manner, modal verbs, lexis related to hobbies, etc.); giving advice (*should / shouldn't*, second conditional, etc.); sequencing ideas (*first, next, then,* etc.)
Secondary focus	Providing an opportunity for learners to use English for self-expression in a personally meaningful context; creating social cohesion and improving group dynamics
Time	2 × 60 minutes
Level	Intermediate
Preparation	You will need a data projector, laptop, mobile phone or other device capable of recording video. An internet connection will be needed to show the clip in Step 1 if this has not been downloaded in advance.

Procedure

1 Tell learners that you are going to show them a clip of someone who has made a career out of a special talent. For example, show learners a video clip of the famous beat box artist Tom Thum. There are many examples on YouTube and he also performed at TEDxSydney (bit.ly/tomthumlimelight).

2 Ask learners to think about a special talent, ability or interest they have and consider how they would answer the following questions. At this point the learners should not reveal anything.

When and why did you start doing this?
What does your family think of your ability / interest?
Is there any special equipment involved?
Is it an innate talent or does it require lots of practice?
Have you ever met anyone else who does the same thing?
What tips would you give someone who wanted to try it?

3 Tell learners to make a 60-second video of themselves demonstrating their talent, ability or interest and to upload the clips to the class channel in time for the next lesson.

4 In the following class the learners present their videos and talk about them, providing answers to the questions they considered in Step 2.

6.2 Meme machine

Outline	Learners pitch ideas for creating a new video meme (see Step 2 for a definition of this term). After a vote, the best idea is created and uploaded to YouTube.
Primary focus	Speaking skills: pitching ideas; describing a process
Secondary focus	Developing media literacy through the dissection, analysis and creation of virally transmitted 'packages of culture' (memes)
Time	2 × 60 minutes
Level	Intermediate and above
Preparation	You will need a data projector, laptop, mobile phone or other device capable of recording video.

Procedure

1 Ask learners what the items in the list below have in common (they are all viral video memes) and what they know about them. The list can be updated with any recent popular memes if necessary:

The Harlem Shake
Rick Rolling
Gangnam Style
Goat Edition
Old Spice Guy

2 Write the words 'meme' and 'viral' on the board and elicit definitions of both terms. If none of the learners are familiar with these words, then explain and provide examples. A 'meme' is a cultural phenomenon or behaviour that is passed from one individual to another, often by imitation. Commonly, it is an image or video that is passed around digitally on the Internet. 'Viral' is the manner in which the memes spread organically and from person to person, in a similar way to a virus.

3 Ask the learners to describe any of the memes they recognize from the list or any meme that might be popular at the time. Encourage them to try to discover the 'DNA' or formula of the meme by breaking it down into its component parts. A good example is the *Harlem Shake*, which can be summarized as follows:

 a approx 30 seconds long
 b always features the same part of the 2012 'Harlem Shake' song by American electronic musician Baauer
 c begins with one person, usually wearing a helmet, dancing alone but surrounded by people who are not paying any attention
 d video cuts to everyone doing the dance (often wearing strange costumes) for the rest of the video
 e video ends in slow motion with the sound of a lion roaring

4 Discuss or brainstorm ideas for what makes a meme spread and become popular. For more ideas on this, Kevin Allocca highlights three possible explanations in his TED Talk, *Why videos go viral* (bit.ly/mememachine).

5 Learners invent and plan a new meme in groups and then pitch their ideas to the rest of the class. Each meme idea must have a set of easy-to-follow steps.

6 Learners vote on the most popular and practical idea and every group creates a video of the new meme. This can be filmed outside of class if necessary or more convenient.

7 Learners upload their meme videos to YouTube and use social media to try to spread the new meme through their networks.

8 After two to four weeks, learners report back on the success or failure of the new meme based on the number of views and any new uploads of the meme by others.

6.3 Voice-over substitution

Outline	Learners transcribe short news reports and then substitute the original voice of the presenter / narrator with their own.
Primary focus	Listening skills; writing; oral fluency; intonation and pronunciation
Secondary focus	Audio recording and editing
Time	2 or 3 × 60 minutes
Level	Intermediate and above
Preparation	Download a collection of recent short news video clips in which voice-overs are used. You will need one video for each group of three or four learners. The *Sky News Headline Update* video podcast is ideal as it is regularly updated and free on iTunes. Each clip lasts three minutes and contains several short news stories. You can find other clips simply by searching for 'BBC one minute world news' on YouTube or by exploring the quirky stories found in the Reuters *Oddly Enough* podcast (although you may require screen-recording software in order to copy the videos to your computer and edit them). Make a second copy of each clip and place it in a different folder. Open the copied files in a video-editing or sound-editing program that accepts video tracks (such as Apple's GarageBand) and remove the audio from the voice-over sections of each clip. Save the files with a new name and then upload both the original and the edited copy to somewhere they can easily be downloaded by your learners (such as Dropbox).

Procedure

1 Ask learners if they have been following the news or are aware of any of the big or unusual stories currently circulating. Find out what they know about each story.
2 Ask learners to form groups of three or four. Show one of the original news clips (with sound) you have downloaded and then write / reveal the following question words on the board:

Who?   *What?*   *Where?*   *Why?*   *When?*   *How?*

3 Check that the learners are able to correctly expand the previous interrogatives into full questions by asking them to brainstorm possible endings. Verify word order and correct use of auxiliary verbs. Possible questions could be:

Who was there?
Why did this happen?
How many people were involved?

4 Play the clip again and ask the learners to take notes on the news stories to answer their questions. Ask them to compare their notes with another group and then gather feedback from the class.
5 Give a pair of links you previously prepared to each group so that they can download both an original news clip and its accompanying edited version with the voice-over removed.
6 Ask the learners to watch the unedited version of their news clip and to transcribe what the presenter / narrator says during the sections in which he or she is *not* visible on screen. This stage could also be done as homework in preparation for the next class, with learners working collaboratively using Google Docs for example. Headphones are recommended if this is to be done in class.

7 Ask each group of learners to individually choose one (or more if there are more stories than group members) of the transcribed stories from their clip and to practise reading it at the same speed as the original presenter. Encourage them to try to imitate the presenter's pronunciation, word stress and intonation at a sentence level. Breaths and any pauses the presenter makes can be marked in the transcript.

8 Give the learners plenty of time to rehearse. When they are ready, they can import the edited news clip (with the presenter's voice-over removed) into their editing software and record their own voices reading the stories. This may take several attempts until they manage to match the speed of their voice-overs with the timing of the news stories.

9 Learners upload their videos to the class channel to share and view each other's work.

6.4 Good game?

Outline	Learners discuss the characteristics that constitute a good video game and record a video review of a game using a green screen background. The green screen is then substituted with images of their gameplay to synchronize with and illustrate their review.
Primary focus	Writing a review; video game lexis; oral fluency; reading
Secondary focus	Increasing critical awareness of video games as new media and analysing them on both structural and aesthetic levels; developing content-creation and video-presenting skills
Time	Around 90 minutes (divided over two classes)
Level	Pre-intermediate and above
Preparation	Learners will need screen-recording software to record their gameplay and video-editing software for Step 12. You will need a video camera or smartphone to film the learners and also a green screen to use as a background in the second class. If this is not available, see 'Variation 1' on page 135.

Procedure

1 Ask learners to consider the following question: *What makes a good video game?*

2 Elicit feedback and then ask the learners to work in pairs or small groups to discuss and rank the following list of game characteristics from 1 to 10 in order of importance:

graphics	*difficulty level*	*controls*	*story*	*multiplayer*
level design	*single player*	*sound*	*originality*	*price*

3 Ask learners to compare their answers with those of another pair or group and then elicit feedback. Select several of the learners and ask them to justify their top and bottom choices.

4 Tell learners that they are soon going to review a game they have recently played, but to first think of a video game they have heard about but not yet played. Instruct them to go online and search for a video review of that game.

5 As learners watch these existing reviews, tell them to note down any words or expressions they think they might find useful when preparing their own review. Encourage learners to try to guess the meaning of any unfamiliar language from the context, but monitor and provide support when requested.

6 Next ask learners to watch their reviews again, but this time they list the themes that are covered rather than any specific language. These will typically include some or all of the following:

- the game genre (FPS, RPG, Puzzle, Racing, etc.)
- presentation and graphics
- the story and objectives
- age restrictions
- difficulty
- information about the publisher or developer
- value for money
- the controls
- music and sound effects

7   Elicit feedback and list the five or six most common themes on the board for learners to note down.

8   Towards the end of the class, tell learners that their homework is to prepare a script for a two-minute video review of a game they have recently played (or they know well). This can be for any platform (smartphones, tablets, PCs, consoles or web-based). The actual review will be recorded in the following class.

9   Reveal the following instructions for preparing the script and go through them to check understanding:

Instructions for video game review

a   Play the game and pause it frequently to take notes.

b   Name the platform, title and publisher of the game.

c   Say which genre the game belongs to and provide a brief overview of the plot. No spoilers!

d   Describe your experience of playing the game with specific examples of things you liked or disliked.

e   Summarize the pros and cons and provide a final rating.

f   Play sections of the game that illustrate the points you make in your review while recording your screen. If this is not possible then download a trailer or gameplay video clip from YouTube. Alternatively, for console games, setting up a smartphone or camera to film the television screen while you play the game can also produce good results.

g   Watch some video reviews of games online and try to imitate the tone and language used as you practise reading your own script.

h   Bring your script and clips of the game to the next class.

From *Language Learning with Digital Video* © Cambridge University Press 2015   PHOTOCOPIABLE

---

10   In the following class allow learners sufficient time to rehearse their scripts a final time. Monitor and provide language support where necessary. Pay special attention to fluency and intonation.

11   Film each learner reviewing their game in front of a green screen. Do not stop the camera if the learners make mistakes while filming their reviews. Just ask them to pick up from the sentence prior to the mistake and continue filming. This way the learners will have a copy of their errors, which they will need to view in order to edit them out of the footage and compose the final version.

12   After each learner has completed their green screen recording, copy the file to their device so that they can begin editing their video and mixing in the clips of their gameplay as a background.

13   When they have completed the editing process, tell the learners to upload their game review videos to the class channel or website so that they can view and comment on each other's work.

Figure 6.1: Student reviewing a game using a green screen

Variation 1

PIP: If a green screen is unavailable, the reviews can be filmed in front of any suitable background (either in class or by the learners themselves outside of class) and then edited together with the screen recording of the game being played. This works best using the picture-in-picture (PIP) effect that enables the learner to insert the gameplay footage inside the main frame. This will appear as a small window right next to them (see Figure 6.2). Using the PIP effect is well suited for larger groups in which it may be impractical to spend two minutes filming each learner in front of the green screen.

Figure 6.2: Student reviewing a game using PIP

Variation 2

Peer review: For Step 8, as part of the homework assignment, learners can use Google Docs to proofread each other's scripts and make suggestions. If you do this, I recommend that each learner corrects at least two other scripts so that there will always be a second opinion.

Variation 3

Film review: By changing the initial question in Step 1 to 'What makes a good film?', and with only small tweaks to the overall procedure, this activity can easily be geared towards learners producing a video film review. Instead of using recordings of gameplay as a backdrop, scenes from their chosen film could be displayed behind them and synchronized with their comments.

6.5 Lip service

Outline	Learners are given a short film clip with the sound removed. They then listen to mixed-up sections of the audio track and try to synchronize them with corresponding moments in the clip.
Primary focus	Listening comprehension skills; speaking skills (negotiating, agreeing / disagreeing, making suggestions, expressing opinions)
Secondary focus	Basic audio-editing skills
Time	30 minutes
Level	Elementary and above
Preparation	You will need a short clip from a film, interview, advert or documentary with the soundtrack separated and mixed up. The audio track can easily be detached in most video-editing software (there is usually a specific menu option for this) and then chopped up using the 'split' command. Some audio-editing tools such as Apple's GarageBand also allow you to import movie clips and detach, split and remix the audio. Laptops or other devices capable of basic audio and video editing will also be needed. These can be shared.

Procedure

1 Tell learners that they are going to do a short listening comprehension activity and that they will need to pay special attention. Play the nonsensical mixed-up audio track and then elicit feedback on what was understood.

2 Learners should spot at least that the recording makes no sense and is out of sequence. Tell them that you can help by showing them the video clip from which the audio was taken. Show the silent clip.

3 Now that the learners have seen the silent video and heard the audio, use the following prompts to ask them to fill in some details regarding what they have understood:

Who appears in the clip?
What are they doing? What are they talking about?
Where are they?
Why are they there?
When do the events take place?

4 In pairs, learners download the silent video clip and scrambled audio track and listen to each section carefully. Provide a realistic time limit (15 to 20 minutes) depending on the length and complexity of the clip. Learners then work together to try to match each section of audio with the corresponding moment in the video clip. This is the stage at which most of the language will be produced as the learners compare what they have understood, express opinions, agree, disagree and make suggestions.

5 When the time is up, show the original clip (with matching sound) for the learners to compare with their own versions.

6 Ask the learners to reflect on how they completed the task and share with the rest of the class what strategies they used to reorder the audio sections. This might include language cues, lip reading, the content of each section of audio, or the visual and contextual clues gleaned from the video.

Note

How similar the learners' versions are to the original is not as important as the discussion they have while working together during Step 4, as the focus of this activity is on the language used during the process of completing the task regardless of the end result.

6.6 Campaign

Outline	Learners create a one-minute video in which they pitch their agenda to become the next leader of their country. These videos are shared, voted on and then the winner declared.
Primary focus	Future tenses; first conditionals; expressing intentions, plans and opinions
Secondary focus	Pitching ideas; raising awareness of verbal and non-verbal rhetorical strategies
Time	30 minutes
Level	Elementary and above
Preparation	You will need video cameras, a video projector, short video clips of iconic speeches (many of these can be found on YouTube), smartphones.

Procedure

1 Play some clips of iconic speeches with the sound off and focus the learners' attention on the body language of the speakers. Ask them to identify any gestures (either clearly intentional or apparently subconscious) used by the speaker. A common example is the closed fist with upward thumb, which is often used as a self-conscious attempt to avoid pointing (a gesture that might be interpreted as aggressive). This has become known as the 'Clinton Thumb', as it was popularized by former US president, Bill Clinton. It is also easy to spot politicians using 'beat' gestures to emphasize their words. You could use categories to provide focus for this observation stage, for example: facial expressions, gestures, eye contact, body posture and movement.

2 Play the clips a second time, this time with the sound on, and ask learners to note any language techniques, expressions or intonation intended to persuade the speaker's audience or add emphasis. For lower-level classes, this step may be supported by transcripts (many of these can be found at The History Place: historyplace.com/speeches/previous.htm). Some examples of language techniques may be the use of future tenses or the first conditional to make promises or express plans and intentions. Strong intonation may be used to communicate conviction, along with dramatic pauses and humour to build or diffuse tension.

3 Tell learners that in the next class one of them will be elected (by their peers) to be the next leader of the country. In order to win the election, they will write a speech in which they outline the actions they will take to improve life for their citizens. Let them know that they will later film themselves delivering their speech and make a one-minute video to be broadcast to their peers. Allow learners 20 minutes to write a first draft while monitoring and providing language support as needed.

4 After learners have written a final version of their speech, they film themselves delivering it, making use of the body language features observed in Step 1. The videos must be edited to fit within the one-minute time limit. They will then be uploaded to the class channel and embedded on a class webpage or blog.

5 Add a poll to the page so that learners can vote for the candidate they consider to be their best next leader.

Follow-up

As a follow-up, the winning candidate's speech may be shown in class and deconstructed, focusing on verbal and non-verbal communication and looking for examples of the techniques observed in Step 1.

Variation 1

Before rehearsing and filming their campaign speeches, learners register for a free English Central account in order to practise mimicking the intonation and body language of some influential speakers.

Variation 2

For slightly lower levels, learners can work in pairs to prepare a speech together. One of the learners will be the candidate for the leadership and the other his or her running mate.

6.7 Structured learning diary

Outline	Over time, learners create a structured portfolio of two-minute video diary entries that encourage them to use and reflect on the language they have learned and the process through which they have learned it. This can be used by both the learner and the teacher to assess and gauge progress and highlight areas that require attention. It also provides a structured way to encourage learners to regularly practise speaking English outside the classroom.
Primary focus	Speaking practice
Secondary focus	Reflecting on learning
Time	Several minutes after each class
Level	Elementary and above
Preparation	You will need a video camera, smartphone or tablet with sound- and video-recording capability.

Procedure

1   Tell learners that after each lesson they are going to make a short video of themselves responding to a different question or instruction. This can either be at home or on the premises, but it *must* be recorded on the same day as they have had an English class. These videos should be between two and five minutes in length.

2   At the end of each lesson, reveal or post the question or instruction on the class webpage or blog. These may be descriptive but the emphasis should be on open-ended prompts that encourage reflection on the language learned, the language-learning process or specific themes connected to the syllabus. Here are a few suggestions:

How do you see your role as a language learner in the classroom?
How do you see the role of the language teacher in the classroom?
What aspects of language learning are easy/difficult for you?
What did you like/dislike about today's class and why?
How confident do you feel about using the language you learned today?
Can you think of a real situation in which the language you learned could be useful?
When you work in a group how much do you usually participate?
How can you improve your listening skills outside the classroom?
Describe and comment on an online learning resource you have used.
What do you think of this statement: 'Learning a language is like learning kung fu.'

3   When they have recorded and edited their videos (there are likely to be false starts and bloopers along the way), learners can either upload and share their video diary entries to the class channel or set up a blog specifically to share their work with the teacher and peers and receive comments and feedback.

7 Medium video creation: Level 2

Several of the activities and projects in this chapter have a particular twenty-first-century slant to them, either by responding to the perceived need for learners to develop specific digital literacies or by attempting to draw attention to skills that might be in danger of becoming neglected or lost. In an 'age of information' when ubiquitous computing and pervasive connectivity are rapidly becoming a reality, information is cheap and plentiful. More than ever, knowing how to collect and *filter* information, synthesize a coherent argument and then express your views are becoming key skills. It is with this in mind that Activity 7.1: *Prove it!* tasks learners with researching the arguments surrounding a controversial statement and then creating a video in which they present either a supporting or an opposing position. These videos are then uploaded to the class channel so that they can be viewed by the other side. This task, in particular, illustrates the usefulness of creating a channel to share your learners' work, as it allows them to view the opposing team's videos in their *own* time and *over* time. As the follow-up homework assignment is to identify 'holes' in the points presented by the opposing team and leave written counterarguments, this asynchrony affords learners the time to think more critically.

Activity 7.2: *Make or break* is also a response to a certain aspect of twenty-first-century life. As Arthur C. Clarke put it, 'any sufficiently advanced technology is indistinguishable from magic', and as technological progress continues to march on at an ever-accelerating rate, most of us have absolutely no idea how any of the 'magic' gadgets around us are made or actually work. This project uses video as a tool for documenting attempts to build or destroy as learners narrate their adventures into the unexplored territory that is all around them.

Activity 7.5: *Detour* extends the theme of exploration in a very literal way. It is becoming increasingly difficult to get lost in twenty-first-century urban environments, whether you're driving or travelling on foot. Cars and phones are often equipped with global positioning technology, detailed built-in maps that can automatically calculate the quickest and shortest route from A to B, and other navigation wonders such as digital compasses that can even tell which way you are facing at any time. Even the effort of discovering new cafés and restaurants can be avoided by asking an app for recommendations and directions based on your location and past preferences. Of course this can improve efficiency and is fantastically useful when you arrive somewhere for the first time, but it can also cement routine and discourage the serendipity and rich sensorial experience of exploring less direct, less efficient alternative routes between the places we frequently visit.

In this mini project, learners learn how to *subvert* these mapping technologies to manually create their *own* routes to explore, using their mobile phones to record and narrate what they discover along the way.

7.1 Prove it!

Outline	Learners form teams and record a video of themselves responding to a controversial statement.
Primary focus	Reading and speaking skills; language for stating opinions, agreeing, disagreeing and sequencing ideas
Secondary focus	Creating and presenting an argument; critical thinking and basic debating skills
Time	Approximately 2 hours
Level	Upper intermediate and above
Preparation	Learners will require internet access for the brainstorming and research stages and a laptop, phone or tablet to edit and upload their video recordings.

Procedure

1   Show learners the following tips (initially without revealing they are for debating) and ask them to guess what subject the tips are for:

> Project confidence, even if you're feeling nervous.
> Get to the point.
> Be respectful and don't make it personal.
> Know your material.
> Anticipate what your opponents might be thinking.
> Show conviction.
> Consider your body language.
> Practise (and then practise again)!
>
> From *Language Learning with Digital Video* © Cambridge University Press 2015   PHOTOCOPIABLE

2   Once it has been established that the tips provide advice for debating, ask the learners to expand on each point by explaining what they mean and why they might be important, and to think of any further points they might add to the list.

3   Write or reveal a controversial statement that the learners can relate to, such as 'Video games are bad for you'.

4   Divide the class into two groups. Choose someone to pick heads or tails and then toss a coin. The winner can choose whether his or her side will be for or against the statement.

5   With a large class, divide each side into smaller subgroups of two or three learners. Set a short time limit (about 15 minutes) and ask learners to brainstorm a list of points that they could make to support their side's position on the statement. Real-time online collaborative whiteboards such as Twiddla (twiddla.com) work well for this stage. When the time is up, each subgroup should choose one of the points to argue. If there are more points than groups, each group can argue more than one point.

6   Tell learners to do some research to help them prepare their arguments and remind them to refer back to the debating tips in Step 1. Often just changing the controversial statement into a question

and then running a Google search will reveal arguments for both sides. For example, in this case searching for 'are video games bad for you?' produces quite a balanced list of results. Encourage your learners to use multiple sources as they gather information and to evaluate each source for credibility.

7   Ask learners to create a short video clip of their group presenting their arguments for or against the statement. With larger groups this can be done out of class or in a quiet spot in the grounds of the building. Smartphones or a simple webcam will suffice for this as long as the sound quality is adequate.

8   Ask learners to upload their videos to the class channel and enable commenting. As a homework assignment, ask them to identify weaknesses in the points presented by the opposite side and add (respectful) written counterarguments.

Follow-up

Select some of the videos to analyse with learners in class, judging how well they followed the advice provided in the debating tips.

Note 1

Once the videos have been shared on the class channel, you can use them as listening material for other classes, who can also vote for the team they think did the best job of supporting their stance.

Note 2

Other interesting topics for debate can easily be found online, for example, at the International Debate Education Association site (idebate.org/debatabase).

7.2 **Make or break**

Outline	Learners create a video of themselves in the process of either making something or taking something apart piece by piece.
Primary focus	Describing a learning process; following instructions; talking about what you plan to do, what you have done and what you are going to do next; reflecting on what has been learned
Secondary focus	Promoting creativity and reflection
Time	15 minutes + 60 minutes
Level	Intermediate and above
Preparation	Each learner will need a smartphone or camera, although these can be shared if necessary as filming will be intermittent. Other equipment will vary according to what each learner chooses to make or break.

Procedure

1   Towards the end of a class, write the terms below on the board and elicit their meanings. Ask learners if they are nouns, verbs or both. Drill each word and draw attention to the prefixes *un-*, *dis-*, *co-* and *re-*. Elicit the general meanings of the prefixes as well as more words that contain them. Next ask learners to decide which of the words below they associate with making something and which they associate with taking something apart. Allow them to use a dictionary for this phase. When they have finished, ask them to brainstorm other words that could fit into each category, e.g. *cut, break, glue, attach.*

unscrew	assemble	dismantle	connect	fold	remove	stick

2   Divide the class into 'makers' and 'breakers'. Tell the makers that in the next class they are going to make a film documenting their efforts to make something. This should be something that they have never attempted to make before, and something that is tangible (as opposed to digital) and practical to complete in class within around 30 minutes. They can follow printed instructions, use an online 'how-to' or watch a YouTube video that will guide them through it step by step. They will need to bring in any special tools and materials they are likely to need. Tell the breakers that their mission will be to bring something in and make a film documenting their efforts to take it apart, piece by piece, in order to see what's inside and how it works or fits together. Again, instructions can be used to help if necessary and it must be something that is practical to do within 30 minutes. Some suggestions for possible themes:

Makers: *an origami object, a potato clock, the best paper plane, a sock puppet, a puzzle, a bracelet, recycling something old into something new*

Breakers: *a toy, a microphone, a broken phone or gadget, a mechanical alarm clock*

3 Next class, before learners begin their projects, tell them that they should begin by filming and describing the equipment, tools and any other items they are going to be using and that they should pause at each stage of the process in order to film and talk about what they have done and what they plan to do next. Their films should end with their thoughts on how easy or difficult it was and what they think they have learned from the process. Monitor and help with language as necessary and make sure that learners do not get too carried away and forget to document their work. The pausing and filming is likely to extend the 30-minute task to 40 or 50 minutes, so make sure you allow for this.

4 Stop learners ten minutes before the end in order for them to make their final recording to finish their film. When learners have completed this, tell them to edit the clips they produced of each stage together and add titles and credits to their video before uploading it to the class channel.

7.3 Ghostly screencast

Outline	Learners record a narrated screencast* as they write a 50-word horror story; the screencast is available as an archive to be included in a learning portfolio or for diagnostic purposes.
Primary focus	Speaking skills (storytelling, agreeing, disagreeing, negotiating, suggesting); reflecting on sentence construction
Secondary focus	Writing skills (See also 'Note' on page 149 for teacher-related aims.)
Time	Approximately 40 minutes
Level	Intermediate and above
Preparation	Learners will need screencasting software installed on their tablets or laptops, or access to free browser-based software such as Screenr (screenr.com) or Screencast-o-matic (screencast-o-matic.com). This is a good activity to do with a class as Halloween approaches.

* *A screencast is a recording of your computer screen output.*

Procedure

1 Tell your learners about the scariest film you have ever seen, how old you were when you saw it and who you were with at the time. Ask them to form pairs and do the same.

2 Learners brainstorm their thoughts on the ingredients of a good horror film. Choose several groups to read out their lists and see if there are any common themes.

3 Tell learners that it is possible to write a scary horror story in just a few sentences by providing just enough detail to create a scene, and then allowing the reader to fill in the rest of the story with their imagination. Show them the following example and help with any unfamiliar vocabulary. Adapt the language for lower- or higher-level learners.

50-word horror story

I was tucking him into bed when he suddenly looked up and said, 'Daddy check for monsters under my bed'. So I looked underneath for his amusement and see him, another him, under the bed, staring back at me quivering and whispering, 'Daddy there's somebody on top of my bed'.

From *Language Learning with Digital Video* © Cambridge University Press 2015   PHOTOCOPIABLE

---

4 Tell learners that together with their partners they are going to write a horror story that is *exactly* 50 words in length (like the one above) and that they will record the writing, editing and discussion involved as a screencast.

5 Tell learners that before they decide on an idea or begin writing, they should open and start their screencasting software. This way, the final video will include the initial discussion and negotiation of their idea, as well as the process of them writing it. Provide a 20-minute time limit.

6 As learners plan and write their horror stories, monitor and provide language support. Initially encourage them not to worry too much about the 50-word target but to aim for something close to this. Once they have a story in place they can adjust the length by deciding what language they can add or remove. The important thing is that they leave the screencast software recording

throughout the creation and editing phases. When they have reached the 50-word target, they can stop the recording.

7 Tell learners to share their screencast videos on the class channel and, for homework, to read each other's stories (they can simply skip to the end of each clip to do this). Embed the videos and a poll on the relevant class page so that they can vote on which one they think is the scariest.

8 Several of the stories are likely to have missed the 50-word target or to have reached it through inaccurate use of language. As an optional follow-up, display several of these stories and work on them as a whole class.

Note

In this activity the point of the video is to provide the teacher with an archive of the language produced by individual learners during the completion of the tasks. This can be used for formative assessment, either as part of a learning portfolio, to inform pronunciation work or focus on common errors. Observing the process by which the learners eliminate language to confine their stories to the word limit will, for example, reveal a lot about how well they understand syntax.

7.4 Game on

Outline	As they play, learners make an on-the-fly video recording describing a video game and the strategies they use to win. They also provide tips to novice players.
Primary focus	The language that emerges from this activity will vary greatly depending on the learners' level and the genre of game they are playing. The main goal here is to allow learners to use their language skills in order to freely communicate about something they find highly motivational and personally engaging.
Secondary focus	Oral fluency; writing a narrative; video game vocabulary; giving advice; playing games more reflectively by actively expressing tacit knowledge
Time	45 minutes (first class), approx 10 minutes (homework), 45 minutes (second class)
Level	Elementary and above
Preparation	Learners will need a laptop, desktop or other device that will allow them to play a video game and make a screencast with sound. Free solutions include browser-based software such as Screenr (screenr.com) or Screencast-o-matic (screencast-o-matic.com) as well as software that needs to be installed such as Quicktime and Ezvid. Alternatively, good results can be achieved by just setting up a camera or smartphone to film the screen and record the live narration. This low-tech option also resolves the problem of recording gameplay on consoles, which do not permit users to install screen-recording software. A data projector is needed for the follow-up in the second class.

Procedure

1 Begin the class by telling a short story based on a video game from a first-person perspective. Do not reveal that it is from a game at this point. Here's an example:

> I couldn't have been more than seven or eight years old. I woke up in the middle of a dark forest with no idea of how I got there. There was a dim light that made everything seem flat and a grey mist that made everything look ghostly and dreamlike. My sister was nowhere to be seen. I panicked and started running. I had to find her. The forest was a dangerous place, full of ditches and traps, but I kept running and climbing onward until I saw it for the first time. Its long black legs dangled from a tree, as sharp as needles. I froze.

The above example is a description of how a game called *Limbo* begins (bit.ly/gameonlimbo). Although *Limbo* has a scripted story, more abstract games such as *Tetris* can easily be turned into a first-person narrative. Imagine, for example, what it would be like to be trapped at the bottom of a pit with an unstoppable shower of geometric debris raining down on you! Ask the learners if they can guess where the story came from. If not, provide more clues and reveal the answer.

2 In pairs or small groups, ask learners to speak about the kind of games they play. They can use the following questions as prompts:

What is the name of the game?
What type of game is it?
What device do you play it on?
Who do you play with or against?
Do you play online or offline?
How good are you at the game?
How often do you play it?
How long does a game usually last?

3 Select several learners to share what they discussed with the rest of the class and then tell them that they are going to write a short first-person narrative (as in the example) based on a game of their choice. This need only be a paragraph in length. Set a time limit of 15 minutes and ask the learners not to reveal which game their story is based on. Monitor and assist with language as necessary.

4 When the time is up, ask learners to read out their stories so that the rest of the class can try to guess which games they are based on.

5 Now explain to your learners that their homework is to play a video game and record a video of their gameplay. At the beginning of their recording, they should introduce and describe the game and explain what genre it is (puzzle, first-person shooter [FPS], role-playing game [RPG], real-time strategy [RTS], etc.). As they play they should describe what they are doing and why. This should be as detailed as possible, including any in-game tactics and strategies they like to use and tips for novice players. The videos should be between three and five minutes long and should be uploaded to the class channel when they are ready. An example recorded by one of my adult learners can be found here: bit.ly/gameonexample

6 In the following class, learners can project their videos on the screen (with the sound turned off) and narrate their gameplay in person to the rest of the class. Encourage the audience to raise their hands to ask questions about anything they saw the player doing that was not explained. The speaker can pause the video to answer before continuing with the narration.

Follow-up

Ask learners to watch the gameplay videos on the class channel, choose one of the games they are already familiar with or would like to know more about, and leave a question or comment.

7.5 Detour

Outline	Learners create a video documenting their experience of taking an alternative route to their place of study or work.
Primary focus	Describing sights, sounds, people, places, directions and experiences
Secondary focus	Promoting creative thinking and mindfulness by disrupting routine
Time	30 + 60 minutes
Level	Elementary and above
Preparation	You will need a video camera, smartphone or tablet with sound- and video-recording capability, an internet-connected device that can access Google Maps online and a Google account. If you are not experienced with using Google Maps you should run through the route-planning stages (Steps 2–8) before your class so that you can demonstrate the procedure as you explain it. It may appear complicated on paper but it takes only 10 minutes in practice.

Procedure

1 Ask learners to find a partner and take it in turns to describe the route they take to school or work each day and what they see along the way.

2 Tell learners to open Google Maps (maps.google.com) on their devices, sign in (if this is not already done automatically) and click on the button that says 'My places', then 'Create map' and then 'New map'. If you have an internet-connected device and a data projector, demonstrate each step as you give the instructions.

3 Instruct learners to give their new map the title 'Detour' and then to zoom in and locate the place where they live, identifying it by dropping a place marker. This can be done by clicking on the balloon icon, moving the cross that appears to the precise spot and then clicking once again to drop the place marker there. Clicking on the balloon will open a dialogue box that will enable them to label this marker as 'home'.

Figure 7.1: Place marker from Google Maps

4 Next learners find their place of study or work and drop a second place marker, this time labelling it 'school', 'university' or 'work'. Clicking on the name of the place marker will cause a paint can icon to appear, enabling the learner to change its colour or shape to distinguish it more easily.

5 Using the draw tool, learners now draw the route that they take between these points on the map.

Figure 7.2: Draw tool from Google Maps

6   Once this has been completed, ask learners to draw a second path by adding a detour to the usual route. This can be a minor change, such as simply taking a street that is parallel to the one they normally take, or a more circuitous deviation that twists and loops its way between the two points. Those who drive can instead park earlier or in a different place from usual and draw the new route from their parking spot to their school, university or workplace.

7   Learners click on the new route to label it and change its colour to distinguish it from the usual route taken.

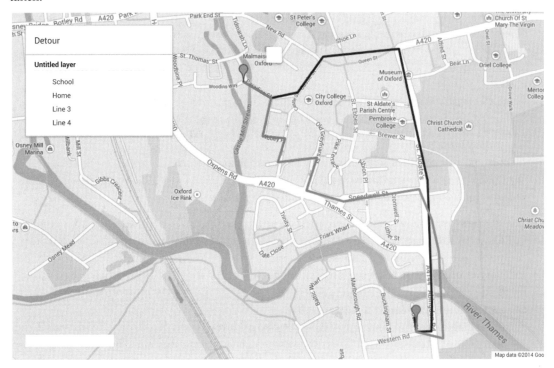

Figure 7.3: Google Map showing two routes

8   Tell the learners to click on the 'Share' button in the top right-hand corner to send their completed maps to themselves by email so that they can print them or keep a copy on their mobile devices.

9   Next time the learners travel between the two points, they attempt to follow the alternative route as closely as they can. As they proceed, they use their mobile devices to film, describe and narrate the new things they see, hear and discover along the way. When they arrive, learners share their video with the class and talk about the new things they experienced on their detours.

Note 1

Younger learners who are driven to school can simply ask their parents to drive the alternative route while they film and narrate their videos through the car window. Public transport users can plan to leave a stop or station earlier.

Note 2

Google and the Google logo are registered trademarks of Google Inc., used with permission.

7.6 Alternative use

Outline	Learners film their partners describing as many alternative uses for an everyday object as they can within a time limit.
Primary focus	*Could / can*; gerunds and infinitives (*you can use a … to* + infinitive, *you can use a … for* + gerund); conditionals
Secondary focus	Promoting divergent thinking and communicative flexibility
Time	30–45 minutes
Level	Elementary and above
Preparation	You will need a video camera, smartphone or tablet with sound- and video-recording capability, data projector and a clock or online timer.

Procedure

1 Write the word *creativity* on the board and elicit definitions from the learners. Open a discussion on the theme of creativity by asking your learners to share their views on the following questions:

Are some people more creative than others?
Is creativity something you are born with or something you learn?
What jobs do you think require creativity?
Do you think you are a creative person? How do you know?

2 Tell learners that you are going to put their creativity to the test. In pairs decide who is going to be Learner A and Learner B. Tell all the As to take out their phones or video cameras (a laptop equipped with a webcam and built-in microphone would also be fine). Explain that you are going to reveal an image of an everyday object and that all the As are going to film their partners as they try to describe as many non-obvious uses for the object as they can within two minutes. Learner A cannot speak or stop filming during this time.

3 Show an image of a brick and start timing the two minutes. If you do not have a stopwatch, there are many handy browser-based timers that allow you to choose your time limit and set an alarm, such as: bit.ly/timeronline or timeme.com/timer-stopwatch

4 When the time is up, learners exchange roles. This time, show an image of a paper clip and once more start the timer.

5 Learners upload their videos to the class channel and then find a new partner that has the same letter as them (As with As, Bs with Bs). The new pairs watch each other's videos and note down the number of uses their partner came up with.

6 Ask learners to share their totals to discover who is the most creative in the class. Show the winning video to the whole class so that they can confirm that the uses were correctly counted.

7 Ask learners if they think this was a good way to test creativity. Allow a short discussion to develop on the topic and ask learners to suggest alternatives. To finish, show *The Adventures of a Cardboard Box*, a short film in which a young boy's imagination is sparked by inventing dozens of uses for a humble cardboard box that he discovers in front of his house (vimeo.com/25239728).

Note

This activity was inspired by J. P. Guilford's 1967 Alternative Uses Test in which the *number* of responses is only one of the factors used to measure creative thinking. The others are as follows:

Flexibility (categories of responses, e.g. responses that all use a brick as a support for something)
Elaboration (the amount of detail supplied in each response)
Originality (the number of unique responses compared to other people's)

Follow-up

Learners form groups of four. Write the names of some other everyday objects on cards and hand out one card to each group. Provide a short time limit for learners to brainstorm and note down alternative uses for their object. Ask each group to call out the alternative uses they've come up with, while the rest of the learners listen and try to guess which object the group was given.

7.7 Body swap

Outline	Learners work in groups of three. Using their phones, they film each other from the shoulders up, telling a very animated story. They then play the video on their phone while visually aligning it with the body of one of the other group members, who tries to act out the story.
Primary focus	Narrative tenses; exclamations of surprise
Secondary focus	Oral fluency and intonation
Time	30–45 minutes
Level	Intermediate and above
Preparation	You will need two smartphones with video-recording capability.

Procedure

1 Show learners the first line of the story below and the following prompts. Ask them to choose one prompt and try to improvise some of the details of what might have happened, using the five Ws (*Who? What? Where? Why? When?*).

First line:
You're not going to believe this, but the other day …

Prompts:
an absolutely amazing coincidence
something you thought you lost but then discovered that you still had
a series of extremely unlucky events
a series of extremely lucky events
the time you nearly did something that would have had terrible consequences
the biggest spider / snake / rat you've ever seen
how you accidentally stopped a street crime and were considered a hero

2 Ask learners to compose a short (around 30–60 seconds when read aloud) but animated story around their chosen prompt. The more exaggerated and unlikely the story, the better. The only rule is that the first line of the story must be: *You're not going to believe this, but the other day …*

3 Once learners have completed their short stories, tell them to form groups of three and to practise reading their stories aloud to each other. Encourage them to exaggerate their intonation and facial expressions as much as possible. Demonstrate this stage if you feel they might benefit from a model. Once they have done this once or twice, ask them to repeat it again, but this time retelling the story without reading it. They should then summarize their story into just four or five keywords. An example for a story about 'a series of extremely unlucky events' might produce the following words: *alarm, fall, ankle, hospital, fired*. This will assist them in remembering the essentials of the story.

4 Learners take it in turns to film each other from the shoulders up, as they tell their stories in an animated fashion. A plain background will work best and learners should exchange phones for this stage so that the video of them telling their story is recorded on their own device. Once all the stories have been filmed, the phones are returned to their owners.

5   Next, one group member stands between the other two, holds up his or her phone and aligns the image with the first 'Body swap' volunteer (see Figure 7.4 below). This learner then plays the video clip, making sure that the sound on the phone is turned up to the maximum. At the same time, the other learner stands a short distance away from the phone and films the mismatched head and body working in tandem.

Figure 7.4: Learners filming a 'Body Swap' session, Step 5

Learners may wish to film two or three takes until they manage to synchronize their talking heads with the gesticulating bodies to their satisfaction and amusement. This sounds far more complicated in writing than it actually is to do once you have mentally worked out the logistics. The above image, taken of my learners filming a Body Swap session, should help.

Tip: Most smartphones have a built-in accelerometer that enables the device to recognize when it has been turned on its side and automatically rotate the video. Stand-alone vertical cameras may not have this capability and would therefore not be suitable for filming the storytelling heads, as the vertical body of the camera would block out the body of the learner acting out the story with gestures.

Note
This project was inspired by Ze Frank's Body Karaoke mission (ashow.zefrank.com/fun/question/?pid=4).

8 Challenging video creation: Level 3

There is a strong emphasis on developing both video- and audio-editing skills in this chapter, using English *procedurally*, to complete tasks, and also to produce language to form the *content* or output of these tasks. In Activity 8.2: *New news*, for example, learners write scripts to accompany clips from news reports that have had the sound removed, obliging them to infer the content of the stories based only on what they can see. Once they have prepared their scripts, they record them, matching the length and timing of the video. They then use film-editing software to synchronize their audio tracks to the news clips. In a variation to this, the classroom can be turned into a fully fledged news studio by using a green screen to film the learners presenting their news stories, with the video clips playing behind them as a backdrop. Activity 8.3: *Shuffle kerfuffle* is also about editing, treating sections of video as if they were virtual LEGO® bricks. In the same way that learners might reorder a text by recognizing cohesive devices or lexical clues, in this activity they receive a mixed-up series of short clips and are tasked with assembling them into a coherent narrative.

Several other creation projects break down the boundaries of the classroom, either metaphorically or literally. Activity 8.6: *Guest speaker* enables the learners to connect remotely with a professional or subject expert. This is useful for ESP classes and also for bringing authentic, situated language and interaction into the classroom when covering a specific theme. I have invited sales and marketing professionals to speak to my learners when working on a coursebook unit on advertising, as well as artists, musicians and other subject experts according to the profile and interests of my learners and the specific components of the curriculum. As well as providing learners who are studying in non-English-speaking countries with an opportunity to communicate in English with someone other than their teacher, the immediacy and authenticity of engaging with an external subject expert can be extremely motivational. Activity 8.7: *Tube talk* uses the 'magic curtain' of the green screen to bring the London Underground into the classroom, using a soundscape that I recorded specifically for this purpose. The recording provides the stimulus for a writing task that leads to the learners performing a filmed dialogue in front of the green screen and then adding in the background sound and images of the Tube to simulate (quite convincingly) that they are having this conversation in situ. Incidentally, this background recording was made using special stereo microphones, so listening with headphones will provide an immersive, surprisingly realistic, three-dimensional effect for the listener.

You'll have to excuse the pun in Activity 8.8: *Footage*. It was irresistible and actually summarizes the activity in a most succinct way. Using prompt cards, the learners go (on foot) on a footage-seeking mission to collect a shopping list of video shots. This works very well in a bustling city centre but can also be done within the grounds of a school or university. Learners then face the challenge of using these seemingly random pieces of footage to tell a story, employing their full range of video-editing skills to make a short film.

8.1 Continuity chaos

Outline	Learners recreate a scene from a famous film while inserting as many continuity errors as possible.
Primary focus	Speaking skills; lexis related to film production
Secondary focus	Listening skills and transcription
Time	2 × 60 minutes
Level	Upper Intermediate and above
Preparation	You will need a clip from a film that contains one or more continuity errors. Many examples of these can be found on YouTube. Try searching the site for 'continuity mistakes' or 'continuity errors'. Deliberate and obvious continuity errors have also been used for comedic effect in films such as the Marx Brothers' classic *Duck Soup* (1933). A good example of many continuity errors deliberately inserted into a scene can be found in this clip, between 0.25 and 2.00: youtu.be/_3vQQ3ntVY4. Learners will need headphones for the transcription stage.

Procedure

1 Learners pay close attention to a scene from a well-known film in which there is a continuity error of some sort. If they do not spot the error, let them know what to look out for and show the clip again, pausing at the relevant point if necessary. Explain that this type of error is quite common in film production as scenes are often shot out of chronological sequence.

2 Ask the learners to think of other kinds of continuity errors and then show them the following error categories. Add any new ones that were elicited.

people   *places*   *clothing*   *plot*   *props*   *environment*

3 Ask learners to illustrate each of the categories with one or more examples. With people, places, clothing and props, it is usually a question of someone or something appearing, disappearing, changing position, etc. Plot errors can happen when a character says something that is contradicted later in the story. Environmental errors can be changes in weather, the direction or length of shadows or something appearing in the landscape that doesn't belong there.

4 Ask learners to form small groups and to search online for a short film scene that they think they could recreate. Scenes with fairly generic backgrounds and with casually dressed characters are usually the easiest.

5 Once they have chosen a scene, they should decide who will play each character. It's okay if there are more learners in the group than characters in the scene, as two or more learners can share the same character (introducing a major continuity error!).

6 Ask learners to listen carefully to their character's speech and to transcribe what they say. This will be easier if they wear headphones. Provide help and support where necessary. If time is short, they can search for the scripts online.

7 Once each member of the group has completed their transcript, give them some time (about 20 minutes) to rehearse their parts. Tell them to refer back to the original clip for a pronunciation and intonation model.

8　Ask learners to consider what type of continuity errors they might introduce into their version of the scene and to make a list. These could be as subtle as the amount of liquid in a glass changing or as obvious as a different person playing the character after a cut. The more errors they can squeeze in the better. This stage is likely to produce large amounts of emergent language, and errors should be noted and / or corrected and help provided as necessary.

9　If space is available, learners can film their scenes in class or on the grounds of the school or campus. If not, they will need to arrange a time and place to do so. If the scene takes place outside, the action can be filmed in class using a green screen and then film or photographs can be taken of a suitable off-site location and used as a backdrop. Similarly, stills from the original film can also be used as background to lend authenticity.

10　Learners upload their scenes to the class channel and list all the continuity errors they spot in each other's clips. This can be done either orally in class or by leaving written comments on the class channel.

8.2 New news

Outline	Learners watch silent news clips, discuss what the stories could be about and write scripts. They then record their news stories and add the audio tracks. This project would be a great way to extend and consolidate the work done in Activity 6.3: *Voice-over substitution* or as a more challenging substitute for advanced learners.
Primary focus	Speaking skills (fluency, intonation, language for agreeing, disagreeing, interrupting and speculating); writing (preparing a script, journalistic lexis); grammar (the narrative tenses, reported speech, use of the present perfect to introduce new or recent actions and events)
Secondary focus	Using visual cues to aid language comprehension
Time	2 × 60 minutes
Level	Advanced
Preparation	Download several short, preferably old, news video clips in which voice-overs are used. YouTube is a good source for these (search for 'news clip'). If older clips are difficult to find, then choose clips containing stories that are unusual. Reuters' *Oddly Enough* podcast is a good source for these (uk.reuters.com/news/oddlyEnough). The important thing is that they are not likely to be familiar to your learners. Another useful source is the *Sky News Headline Update* video podcast on YouTube.

Open each clip in a video-editing program and remove the audio from the voice-over sections of each clip. Leave the introductory music and parts in which the news presenter is on camera. Save the files with a new name and then upload the edited copies to somewhere they can easily be downloaded by your learners (such as Dropbox).

An internet connection, laptop/tablet and data projector are necessary for Step 2. A green screen is needed for the Variation. |

Procedure

1 Tell learners that, as with reading a text, it is not necessary to understand everything in a video in order to get the gist of what's happening. In fact, paying attention to the context, the place, the people present, their facial expressions and the things the camera focuses on can greatly assist learners to attach meaning to the language they hear.

2 Open a news website that contains streamed video content. Turn the sound off and explain to learners that they are going to watch a silent news story and will have to guess what it is about, where it takes place and who is involved or affected by the events.

3 Begin playing the clip and encourage learners to take notes of what they think the story is about.

4 Gather feedback and ask learners what visual cues they used to draw their conclusions and piece together the news stories.

5 Ask learners to form small groups (the number in each group should ideally correspond to the number of news stories contained in each clip). Provide each group with a link to download an edited news clip with the sound removed.

6 Ask learners to watch their clips several times and to discuss and take notes on what they think each story is about, where it took place and who was involved, etc. Once they have agreed on the basic content of each story, they can begin working on transforming their notes into scripts.

7   Once the scripts are ready, learners can begin to rehearse reading their stories, synchronizing their pace with the video clips. Provide help with pronunciation and intonation as necessary.

8   Learners open their video clips in their video-editing software and record their voice-overs. This can be done in short sections to make it easier to avoid errors and maintain the correct pace to match the video track.

9   Learners merge their new audio tracks containing their voice-overs with the video track and export the finished video to the class channel to share.

Variation

To increase the focus on presentation skills and oral fluency, learners film themselves presenting the news or weather forecast in front of a green screen. Using video-editing software, silent video clips can then be dropped in as backgrounds to create the effect of an authentic television news program. iPads can be used as teleprompters to assist with longer sequences. An example of this can be viewed here: youtu.be/tBO3fDqxYWs

Figure 8.1: Learners presenting a news broadcast and a weather forecast

8.3 Shuffle kerfuffle

Outline	Learners watch a mixed-up video narrative and then cut and reorder it using video-editing software.
Primary focus	Speaking; linking words and other cohesive devices (*so, because, but, though, first, after that,* etc.); deictic language (*here, now, then, there, this, those,* etc.); agreeing and disagreeing; justifying opinions
Secondary focus	Developing editing and listening skills
Time	60 minutes
Level	Elementary and above
Preparation	Learners will need a laptop or tablet with video-editing software installed (one for each pair of students) and access to a short, pre-prepared video file. Select a video clip that is appropriate for the age and language level of your learners. If possible, choose something that contains a story with a clear start, middle and end. This can be a section of an animated film, a few minutes of a documentary, a TV advert or something original recorded by the teacher. Download and import the video into your editing software, keeping a copy of the original. Split the clip into multiple sections (the more sections, the more difficult the task will be), but choose strategic points to make these cuts. Places in which there is a scene change generally work best. Once you have made your cuts, shuffle them by dragging and dropping each section to a different place in the timeline and then export the mixed-up pieces as a single, whole video clip. Upload this to a file-sharing service for your learners to download in class.

Procedure

1 Tell learners that you are going to show them a video clip that tells a story. Play the clip and then choose someone to recount what he or she saw. The learner is likely to have considerable difficulty in achieving this task, so after a short time interrupt and explain (if this is not already obvious by now) that the clip has been reshuffled.

2 Tell learners that, in pairs, they are going to edit the video to return the shuffled clip to a coherent story (not necessarily the original one) within 30 minutes.

3 Provide learners with the shuffled clip, making sure that all pairs have the file before starting.

4 Learners import the file into their video-editing software and watch the clip again, discussing and deciding where to cut and reposition sections in order to produce a coherent story. As the learners engage with the task, create a 'making of' video by moving around the class and filming their discussions, debates, decisions and negotiations, but do not interfere unless specifically asked for help with language.

5 When the time is up, learners export their reordered story as a single whole clip and share it on the class channel.

Figure 8.2: Example of a shuffled video clip

Follow-up
The 'making of' video from Step 4 can be uploaded to the class channel for the learners to watch and reflect on in a subsequent class. This record of language in use can also be used to identify communication breakdowns and language errors to tackle in the future.

Variation
When preparing the video for more advanced learners, you can make multiple cuts *within* a scene, dividing sentences at the points in which specific cohesive devices (such as linking words and pronouns), collocations or multi-word verbs are used.

8.4 That was then

Outline	Learners research how people lived 100 years ago and create narrated video reports explaining and comparing the differences between then and now.
Primary focus	Describing and comparing the past and present
Secondary focus	Researching and creating a report
Time	30 minutes + 60 minutes
Level	Intermediate
Preparation	Learners will need access to internet-connected devices for the research stage and a camera-equipped mobile phone or camera to record video of present-day places and practices. Video-editing software is needed to compose and narrate the final video report.

Procedure

1 Show learners several important events that took place 100 years ago. Typing a year into Wikipedia will provide a list of events divided by month. You can also search sites such as HistoryOrb.com by year. Ask learners to find a partner to discuss and try to agree on which year all of these events might have taken place. Here are some examples from 1914:

Henry Ford introduces assembly line for Model T-Fords
First successful blood transfusion
First full-colour film shown
First electric traffic light is installed
World War I began

2 Once it has been established that these events took place a century ago, ask learners to research and collect information to answer questions about what life was like back then. This information should be a mixed-media combination of images, text, audio and video clips. You will need one question for each pair of learners. Provide a time limit and tell them to save their files. They will need them next class. Some example questions:

How did people communicate back then?
How did people take and share photos?
How did men shave?
What and where did children play?
What jobs did people do?
What were classrooms like?
What was in the news?
How did people receive their news?
What was in fashion?
Who was famous and for what?

3 Once learners have collected sufficient information about the past, ask them to pair off with another group and share their findings.

4 Tell learners that for homework they are each going to make an *original* (i.e. using their own cameras rather than found media) two-minute film to find out the answer to the same question, but for the present day. This video can have sound, but should not be narrated at this point.

5 Next class, ask learners to work with the same partner and import both of their short films into the video-editing software on one device. They will now edit together scenes from both of their short films about the present day, making use of the best shots and cutting anything they don't need. The end result must be a one-minute film. Although having two different sets of footage shot from different angles and in different places should lead to a better-quality, more documentary-like feel, the primary goal here is for the learners to produce language as they negotiate which clips to cut and which to keep, in order to merge their four minutes of footage into just one minute.

6 Once they have combined their films, they can then select and import the images, audio and video clips about the past that they collected in the previous class into their video-editing software and organize them into a logical sequence *before* their one-minute clip.

7 When they are happy with the result, ask the learners to write a script in order to record a voice-over narrating the entire film. For the section describing the past, they can use the text they found in Step 2 as a starting point. Provide language support when requested.

8 When the scripts are ready, learners record their voice-over narrations. These should alternate in order to give all the learners an opportunity to speak about both the past and the present.

9 Learners upload and share their videos on the class channel.

8.5 Dub club

Outline	Learners write scripts and film themselves performing short scenes. The audio is removed and a different group have to guess what is being said and then create and dub their own dialogue.
Primary focus	Planning and writing a script; agreeing and disagreeing; making suggestions
Secondary focus	Producing context-appropriate language
Time	2–3 hours in class (+ work done outside the classroom)
Level	Elementary and above
Preparation	You will need a short clip from a silent film, a bag or box of context cards (see Step 3), video- and sound-recording/editing equipment such as smartphones, tablets or laptops for the learners to produce and edit their video creations. Most silent films can now be freely used. An excellent source is The Internet Archive (archive.org/details/silent_films). The first two minutes of *Mabel's Blunder* (1914) work well (archive.org/details/MabelsBlunder1914).

Procedure

1 Explain to learners that you are going to show a clip from a film, and that they will need to pay special attention and take notes because afterwards they will have to tell you what was said.

2 Show a short clip (a minute or so should suffice) of a scene from an old silent film. Ask the learners to tell you what was said in the clip (nothing!). Ask them to imagine what the characters *might* be saying if there were sound and play the scene again, pausing regularly. Encourage the learners to pay attention to the non-verbal cues that help to contextualize the communication between the characters, such as the scenery, set, props, costumes, lighting, gestures, posture, facial expressions and relative positions of the actors. Elicit feedback.

3 Learners form groups of two to three. Ask one member of each group to pick a context card from the bag or box. The information written on the card can *only* be revealed to the other members of the group. Here are some suggestions for possible contexts:

a minor road accident
a complaint about the food in a restaurant
bumping into a stranger
a marriage proposal
mistaken identity

4 Tell learners that, in their groups, they are going to film a short scene based on the context written on their card, but that first they will need to prepare a script. Provide a 30-minute time limit to prepare the scripts. Monitor and provide language support as needed.

5 Learners arrange to film their scenes outside of class, both to prevent the other groups from hearing their dialogue and to find a suitable setting, clothing and props. When they have finished cutting and editing their scene, instruct them to make a copy, remove the sound and then export their scene as a silent film. The learners then upload these silent versions to the class channel before they return next lesson.

6 In the following class learners exchange their silent film scenes with another group and watch them several times, once again paying attention to any non-verbal cues that may help to reveal the context and what is being communicated.

7 Once they have agreed on the context of the scene, tell learners to watch their clips again, this time pausing and writing the imagined dialogue for each of the characters as they go. Monitor and provide language support as needed.

8 Once the scripts are ready, learners record their dialogue. This can be done using basic audio-recording software or directly within most video-editing software. Once the track has been recorded, it should be added to the film clip and edited so that the spoken dialogue approximately matches the timing of the original scene.

9 Learners present their work to the class, first explaining how they interpreted the video they were given and what visual cues informed their ideas. They then show their dubbed versions. The group that produced the original video should present next, but this time they should begin by showing the original recording (with sound) of the dubbed scene presented by the previous group.

Variation 1
Instead of using the context cards and writing original dialogue, lower-level learners can film their scenes based on pre-existing scripts from any film or TV show (many are freely available online, e.g. The Daily Script: dailyscript.com).

Variation 2
If time is short this activity also works well as a stand-alone dubbing exercise. Instead of filming original scenes based on the context cards, groups of learners each receive a clip from a silent film, write their own scripts, record their voices and dub the video using their editing software. *Mabel's Blunder* (see link in 'Preparation' on page 168) can be used for this.

8.6 Guest speaker

Outline	An experienced professional or subject expert is invited to videoconference with learners, who prepare and ask questions, and receive an assignment from the guest speaker. This activity is especially useful for ESP classes or for focusing on the language surrounding a specific theme.
Primary focus	Forming and asking questions; listening comprehension; speaking interaction
Secondary focus	General listening sub-skills (e.g. using paralinguistic clues to infer the meaning of unfamiliar language)
Time	45 minutes + project work
Level	Elementary and above
Preparation	Find a guest speaker who has professional skills, subject knowledge or expertise relating to a theme in the curriculum. In addition, ask your speaker to prepare and send you some brief biodata and an accompanying photograph. You will need a reliable broadband connection, a laptop, smartphone or tablet connected to external speakers and equipped with a microphone. A data projector would be ideal to project the image of the guest speaker onto a larger screen. Skype is the ideal software to use due to its cross-platform compatibility. Videoconferencing software such as Facetime also works well between Apple devices. Screen-recording software will be needed for those wishing to keep an archive of the videoconference (agree that this is okay with the speaker first) to use as the basis of a follow-up lesson. At the time of writing, Skype does not have a built-in way to record video calls, but using a screen-capture program or installing separate software such as Evaer (evaer.com) is an easy workaround.

Procedure

1 Just before the class begins, open Skype (or alternative videoconferencing software) and check that your speaker is logged in. Make a brief connection just to check that the speakers and microphone are working correctly. Place the laptop on a raised surface facing your class so that your speaker will be able to see them. Create some space immediately in front of the camera so that your learners can approach individually to speak to your guest.

2 Inform learners that they are going to receive a special guest in class who is going to talk about the theme you have selected. Reveal an image of the speaker and ask learners to make inferences about his or her possible career based upon their appearance.

3 Reveal the biodata provided by the speaker so that learners can compare what they guessed with the information provided. Encourage learners to guess the meaning of any unfamiliar language in the biodata through context and grammatical clues and then ask them to prepare three questions to ask the speaker directly. Write one or two on the board as examples and encourage open-ended questions rather than those requiring a simple yes/no response, such as:

How did you become a … ?
What do you like about your job?

Write the additional question prompts for lower-level learners:

Who …?   *Where …?*   *When …?*   *Why …?*   *Do/does …?*

4   Provide an appropriate time limit (5 to 10 minutes should suffice). Monitor and assist as learners formulate their questions and get them to practise asking their questions to you in order to assist with pronunciation and intonation. Listen out for duplicate questions and suggest alternatives.

5   Start your screen-recording software, connect with your guest speaker and introduce your class. Allow for a little ice-breaking chat and be prepared to intervene or moderate if conversation becomes awkward, confused or dominated by a particular individual. It is a good idea to remain within camera frame (but off to one side) so that your guest can also see you. This is particularly important if he or she is not an experienced public speaker.

6   Either select or ask for a volunteer learner to approach the laptop, introduce him- or herself and choose one of their questions to ask directly to your guest. When this has been answered, encourage the learner to ask a follow-up question based on the response received.

7   Repeat this process until all of the questions have been asked or the agreed time has run out. When the Skype chat has ended, stop the screen recording and save it to be used as content for a future lesson or to focus on the language produced in a follow-up class.

Note

If you are inviting an international speaker, make sure that time zone differences are resolved. It is also strongly advised that you run a test, preferably at the same time and using the same equipment as you intend to use on the scheduled day, in order to preempt or troubleshoot any technical issues. Also, arrange for your speaker to be standing by in Skype at least 10 to 15 minutes before he or she is due to speak. Provide some background information on your class and ask your speaker to try to speak slowly and clearly if your group is of a lower level. For the Follow-up (see below), you will need to ask your speaker to suggest a project related to the chosen theme.

If you do not know a suitable English speaker, I recommend using social media to connect with the huge international English language teaching community. They may be able to connect you with a willing speaker or even volunteer themselves. A good place to start would be the ELTChat network: eltchat.org or #ELTChat on Twitter.

Follow-up

Prepare a project related to the theme of the discussion for learners to undertake. The results can be sent to the guest speaker who can either provide a written grade or make a second Skype appearance in order to provide feedback directly to the learners.

After speaking to a sales professional in the UK via Skype, I challenged my learners to produce their own radio show, complete with embedded advertising. You can download and listen to an example here: bit.ly/radioshowads

8.7 Tube talk

Outline	Learners simulate a conversation on the London Underground using a green screen and an audio recording of background sounds.
Primary focus	Informal conversational English; narrative tenses (*going to / will*)
Secondary focus	Developing video-editing skills
Time	Approximately 60 minutes
Level	Elementary and above
Preparation	You will need a video camera, smartphone or tablet with video-recording capability, a green screen, an image taken on the London Underground (bit.ly/tubetalk) and an in-situ audio recording of background noise and chatter (bit.ly/14lrBLZ). Set up the green screen and camera before the class begins.

Procedure

1   Reveal the following clues one by one and ask learners to raise their hands if they can guess the connection between them (they are all related to travelling on the London Underground system). Allow them to use a dictionary if necessary. Once this has been established, elicit more specific connections about each word or expression, such as what each might refer to or describe. For example, *rumbling* refers to the sound of the train accelerating or slowing down and an *Oyster card* is the plastic smartcard that replaced paper tickets.

newspapers	rumbling	obstructing the doors can be dangerous	
Oyster card	beeping	Londoners	crowded
Tube	tunnels	mind the gap	

2   Provide some brief background information about the London Underground or give the learners a five-minute time limit to find out as much as they can about it and report back.
3   Show the background image taken on the London Underground to provide context and then ask learners to close their eyes and listen to the background sounds on the audio recording. When the recording has finished, select several learners and ask them to describe what they heard. Supply a link for each pair of learners to download both the image and the audio file. They will need both of these later.
4   Tell learners to work in pairs and imagine a two-minute conversation they might have as they travel from one station to the next. This should include:

Where they have just been
What they have just done
Where they are going next
Someone they know but who is not there

5   Once they have discussed their ideas, tell them to write a script (conversation prompts should suffice for higher-level learners) and to rehearse performing it. Monitor and provide assistance when needed. If the learners are short of inspiration, they can research what's on in the area of Great Portland Street, which is mentioned in the audio recording. The website LondonTown is a good place to start as it is continually updated with activities based on specific locations: bit.ly/londontownsite.

6   Film each pair of learners performing their 'Tube talks' in front of the green screen. For increased authenticity they can sway from side to side a little as they talk in order to simulate the rocking motion of the train. Allow learners to copy their video files to their own devices for editing. Alternatively, to save time, each pair can be filmed using one of their own smartphones or tablets.

7   Using their video-editing software, learners edit their conversation and then substitute the green screen background for the London Underground image. They then add the audio track of background noise to their clips and export the final film to the class channel for sharing with the rest of the class.

Figure 8.3: Students performing a 'Tube talk'

Note

This image taken on a London underground train can be used as an alternative backdrop. It is freely available in the public domain and can be found at: bit.ly/undergroundimage. For more background information and to improve cultural understanding of the role of the Tube in London, learners can watch clips from *The Tube*, an excellent BBC2 documentary (bbc.in/1n9qhsJ).

Variation

This lesson could be adapted to different contexts. For example, searching for 'airport sounds' on YouTube brings up several audio soundscapes, including one of announcements being made at London's Heathrow Airport.

8.8 Footage

Outline	Learners film footage of specific subjects, then remix their shots to form a narrative, write a script and record a voice-over.
Primary focus	Writing a narrative; speaking skills (exchanging ideas, expressing and justifying opinions, agreeing, disagreeing, suggesting, speculating, evaluating, negotiating); pronunciation; oral fluency
Secondary focus	Lexis related to the video production process
Time	2 hours
Level	Elementary and above
Preparation	You will need prompt cards (see example on page 175) containing the list of shots the learners need to collect. An example card can be downloaded at: bit.ly/footagecard. One smartphone, tablet or other device capable of recording video and sound per learner is preferable, although these can be shared if necessary. A laptop or tablet will be required for the editing phase.

Procedure

1 Towards the end of a class write the words *foot* and *age* on the board and ask learners to explain what they mean. Next ask them how the meanings change when the words are put together to form the word *footage*. If they are not familiar with the term (which is quite likely) after a few guesses, explain that it usually refers to the action or scenes recorded on film (or digitally).

2 Explain that next class there is going to be a video scavenger hunt and that they will need to bring a fully charged device capable of recording video. Agree to meet your learners at a convenient point in a busy area.

3 Hand out the prompt cards and explain that their mission is to try to get as many of the listed shots as possible within the time limit. Allow 20–25 minutes to get the shots on the example card. This is usually enough in a busy urban area, but timing may vary according to the number and type of shots and the place in which learners are searching.

4 Check that learners all understand the language on the cards and agree to meet back at the same spot when the time is up. Send them off to gather their shots. Initially, some learners who are not used to doing activities outside the classroom may linger around the meeting point (and the teacher). Providing an example by taking your own card and walking off filming shots usually encourages them to be more adventurous. And it's fun.

5 When the time limit is up and everyone has arrived back at the meeting point, return to class and allow learners some time to copy their footage from their mobile devices to their laptops if they prefer to edit on a larger screen. It doesn't matter if some learners have not completed the list of shots as seven or eight will usually suffice. Those who used tablets may wish to edit directly on their device if they have a capable application installed.

6 Learners view their footage and use their editing software to remix, cut, paste and add transitions, effects and music in order to create a visual story from their shots. Monitor and ask learners to tell you their stories as they develop. Make suggestions for how different shots might connect to form scenes, and how the scenes might connect to form a broader narrative.

7 When learners have assembled their shots into a final version, tell them that they are going to record and add a voice-over narration to their videos, but that they will first need to script their

stories. While learners could write their scripts individually for homework and email them to the teacher for revision or grading, a collaborative peer review approach can be more motivational and productive. It is very simple to organize this using the 'collaborative revision' feature of Google Docs, and it can make writing less threatening and more engaging in class.

8   At home, learners record their voice-overs using their editing software and upload the finished videos to the class channel.

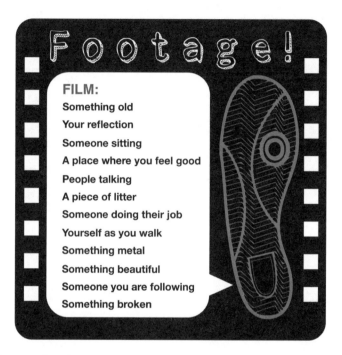

Figure 8.4: Example of a prompt card

Follow-up
In the following class, screen the films. Learners pick their favourite and comment on what they liked about it.

Note
The instructions for this project are geared towards adult learners, as it works best when the participants are able to freely explore an urban area. However, the prompt cards can easily be adapted so that the specific shots can all be found within the school building, grounds or university campus. Make sure you have the necessary permissions and take appropriate precautions (such as having the learners work in groups rather than individually) if you plan to take younger learners outside the school.

Variation
In pairs or small groups, learners can prepare their own prompt cards and then exchange them with another group. Make sure that these include a reasonable number of shots (10 to 12 is fine) and that they are practical to capture within the time available.

9 Elaborate video creation: Level 4

While 'elaborate' may be a fitting adjective to describe the tasks in this chapter, I am by no means using it as a synonym for 'difficult'. These tasks are elaborate in the sense that they contain a wide variety of sequential components or stages. Some of them extend into medium- or long-term projects. For this reason they may be better suited for teachers and learners who have already 'levelled up' by developing their technical, creative and project-management skills while working through some of the earlier activities. Activity 9.8: *Coming up ...*, for example, tasks the learners with writing, creating, editing and sharing their own television shows, complete with introductory theme music, titles and green screen effects. Only a short time ago, this would have required prohibitively expensive, specialized hardware and software. Now, many of the learners are carrying around powerful, multi-purpose television studios in their pockets.

Activity 9.7: *Half-baked remake* is one of the most creatively elaborate projects as the learners produce (deliberately bad) remakes of famous Hollywood blockbusters. Activity 9.6: *Invader* is an example of a *pervasive mobile game*. Pervasive games extend gameplay beyond the typical boundaries of play such as boards (e.g. Scrabble), courts (e.g. tennis) or screens (e.g. video games) and into the real world. They are sometimes described as 'games that surround you', as the lines between the game world and the real world become blurred. I designed this game to provide a context for learners to use English outside the relatively sterile confines of the classroom, to engage with people, places and objects in a more situated and embodied manner. This is especially important for learners in non-English-speaking countries. The game places the learners in the role of aliens who have just arrived on Earth. They are on a pre-invasion reconnaissance mission to study human behaviour, places and objects, and so must try to blend in as they use their mobile devices to record on-the-fly video reports and document their observations.

I originally designed this game to use with the extremely large groups of mixed-ability learners I was teaching at a university. The classrooms were designed for lecture-style teaching, and so both the physical surroundings and the sheer number of learners made communicative language teaching quite a challenge. After running the first play test with a group of more than 50 learners, it became clear from the videos that more language was produced by each individual during one hour of gameplay than would have otherwise been possible in a whole semester. The game also revealed the enormous amount of creative and imaginative thinking being done by the learners, as they postulated that the circular iron manhole covers they were observing might be an advanced network of teleportation devices, enabling 'the humans' to traverse the city at great speed, or how the curious habit of smoking might be part of some kind of religious ritual. Since then, the game has taken on a life of its own, with versions being set up by teachers in several countries around the world.

9.1 I, Object

Outline	Learners record and narrate a video diary from the perspective of an inanimate object.
Primary focus	Writing and narrating a descriptive first-person narrative (greater focus can be placed on the discussion, writing or narration stages and on specific vocabulary or tenses according to the needs and abilities of the learners)
Secondary focus	Developing digital editing skills; encouraging empathy and creative thinking
Time	35 minutes (first class) + 60 minutes (second class)
Level	Upper Intermediate and above
Preparation	You will need a smartphone or other portable device with video-recording capability and a laptop or tablet with basic video- and sound-editing software such as Apple iMovie or Windows Movie Maker. Many modern smartphones can also handle the editing stage, although the relatively small screen sizes of these devices can complicate the process. A roll of masking tape is also useful (see 'Note' page 179). The example script for Step 2 is available at: bit.ly/iobjectscript and the example diary entry for Step 3 can be found at: youtu.be/cOloeAuK-v4

Procedure

1 Draw or show the class images of everyday household or classroom objects, e.g. door, television, sock, pencil case, etc. Focus on one and ask the following questions, encouraging learners to freely brainstorm ideas:

   What can this thing do?
   Where does this object usually live?
   What might it be able to see from there?
   What kind of personality might this object have?
   What might this object think about?
   What would it be like to be this thing?

   For example, in the case of a door, it can open and close, allow or block entry, squeak, slam, jam, hide, reveal, or protect what's inside. Encourage learners to be as imaginative as possible at this stage.

2 Reveal the script written from the perspective of an everyday object (see 'Preparation' above) and ask learners to suggest what that object might be. Encourage them to guess the meaning of any unfamiliar vocabulary and to look for clues in the text that might help to identify it. Do not confirm or deny any of the suggestions but ask learners to justify their answers.

3 Show the example diary entry filmed from the perspective of a kitchen toaster (see 'Preparation' above) and then ask the following questions, encouraging discussion:

   What was the noise that woke it up?
   What was the shadow and why was it too fast to see clearly?
   Why does the toaster get so angry over such a small thing?
   Why did its attempts to calm down fail?
   Why did its vision become blurred when it began to lose control?

4   Tell learners that they are going to make their own *I, Object* diary entries from the perspective of an object of their choice. This stage of the project will take place at home. To do this, first they will need to use their phones or alternative devices to record a short video clip from the point of view of their chosen object. The length of the video can be increased according to the language abilities of the learners, but I suggest something between 1 and 2 minutes. At this stage the recording will not have any narration.

5   Next class, learners bring in their clips and work on writing their narration scripts. Provide help, feedback and suggestions when appropriate. The amount of writing will vary in accordance with the length of the clip the learner produced.

6   Learners practise reading their scripts aloud and, at this point, help with pronunciation and intonation should be provided. Select two or three learners to read their scripts to the rest of the class who must try to guess which object's point of view is being expressed.

7   At home, learners record their audio narration and add it to their video clip. When they are happy with their work they can upload it to a video-sharing service (e.g. Vimeo or YouTube) and email the link to the teacher, or they can upload it to the class channel to share.

Note

In order to capture the selected object's point of view, I often use a few strips of masking tape to attach my phone or camera directly to the object.

I would encourage teachers to work through the procedure and create an object diary entry themselves before doing this with a class. This will highlight any potentially problematic timing or technical issues.

Follow-up

Once learners have successfully completed this activity, it can easily be repeated as an ongoing homework project or portfolio piece, with learners producing multiple diary entries for different objects over time.

9.2 Corruption disruption

Outline	Learners film themselves telling the missing parts of a story in order to complete a video narrative that has been damaged due to data loss or interference.
Primary focus	Speaking fluency; storytelling; listening; writing; pronunciation
Secondary focus	Developing digital-editing skills
Time	2 × 60 minutes
Level	Intermediate and above
Preparation	You will need a bad disguise, a smartphone or other portable device with video-recording capability, a short video you have produced yourself, and a short video clip of static interference. There are many free clips of video static available online (e.g. bit.ly/loopingstatic). The learners' video-recording stage of this activity can take place either in class or at home. Laptops or tablets will be required for the editing stage.

Choose or write a short story that matches the level of your learners. Shaggy-dog stories work well as they are usually quite rambling and full of inconsequential detail. Ghost stories are also good. The important thing is that it is not likely to be familiar to the learners.

Set up a camera and put on your bad disguise (this can be as simple as a hat and sunglasses, but is necessary as you're claiming not to know the source of the video!). Film yourself telling the complete story from start to finish. Begin with an introduction that will engage your learners' imaginations such as, 'You won't believe what happened to me the other day'.

Make a copy of the recording, play it back and select parts of the story to cut out. These can be important plot elements, descriptive sections or parts in which a specific tense is used. To make it more convincing, these cuts should be untidy – taking place mid-sentence. You should cut enough so that only the skeleton of the original story is left.

Replace each of the parts you cut with a clip of video static. This can be copied and pasted to increase the time of each gap in the story. The effect should be of a 'corrupted' video with chunks of static mixed in with the bare bones of the original story. When you have completed this stage, upload the video to a cloud service or the class channel so it can be downloaded by your learners.

Procedure

1 In class, explain to learners that you have found a video file on an old laptop but that the data has become corrupted and it no longer plays correctly. Show them the clip containing all the static interruption and ask them for their help in reconstructing the narrative. Brainstorm thoughts on what the story could be about and ask learners whether they think it has a happy or tragic ending.

2 Learners download the clip to their devices. In pairs, small groups or individually, they then work on scripting the missing sections of the narrative.

3 Next, learners film themselves telling the missing parts of the story and interweave their own clips with the original video, removing the static to create an 'uncorrupted' video story.

4 Ask learners to upload their versions of the story to the class channel or another video-sharing service. Learners view and compare each other's recreated stories.
5 Finally, play back the original uncorrupted version of your story so learners can compare their versions with it.

Follow-up
Reshuffle: Learners can create new versions of the story by remixing sections of their own clips with those of other learners.

Variation
This project can easily be shortened or adapted to lower levels by only removing the end or middle of the story during the pre-class preparation of the corrupted video.

9.3 Trope

Outline	Learners create 1950s American-style TV commercials for modern-day consumer products.
Primary focus	Oral fluency; intonation; language related to product description and advertising (use of adjectives, comparatives, superlatives, the imperative, alliteration, hyperbole, rhyme, etc.)
Secondary focus	Developing media literacy skills through the identification of common advertising tropes, stereotypes and production techniques; identifying habitual errors. This activity can also be used to focus on specific language points such as word order with adjectives.
Time	1–2 hours
Level	Intermediate and above
Preparation	Find some clips of 1950s TV adverts, plus two video clips of adverts for the same product, one modern and one from the 1950s or 1960s. A collection of public domain 1950s–1960s adverts can be found on the Internet Archive (archive.org/details/Televisi1960). Alternatively, a YouTube search for '1950s USA TV commercials' will produce many examples. A smartphone or other portable device with video-recording capability will be needed as well as laptops or tablets for the editing stage.

Procedure

1   Show a clip of a vintage TV advert from the 1950s or 1960s. Ideally, this should be of a product that still exists. Next show a modern advert for the same (or a similar) product.

2   In pairs or small groups, ask learners to identify as many stylistic changes between the old and new advert as they can. Show the two clips a second time for them to take notes based on their observations of some the following elements:

Features of old and new adverts

hairstyles	length of advert
fashion	ages of actors
jingles / soundtracks	amount of speaking
stereotypes	style of language
how often product is shown	aspects of editing (many or few cuts?)
how often product is mentioned	number of camera angles used
location of shots (mostly inside or out?)	black and white / colour
sophistication of message (direct 'buy this!' or more abstract?)	logos

From *Language Learning with Digital Video* © Cambridge University Press 2015   PHOTOCOPIABLE

---

3   Elicit feedback from learners and ask some follow-up questions. Generally they will notice the relative simplicity, repetitiveness and naivety of the older advert.

4   Tell learners that their groups are going to make a TV advert for a modern product of their choice, but that this advert will be in a 1950s / 1960s American style.

5   Provide learners with the link to the Internet Archive's collection of old broadcast advertising (see 'Preparation' above) and allow about 15 minutes for them to browse through some examples.

6 Ask them to choose the modern equivalent of the product they would like to advertise in their group, avoiding repetition if possible, and then set a time limit (about 20 minutes) for them to work on their scripts, using the example adverts as a model. Each member of the group must have a speaking role in the advert. Encourage learners to think about where the dialogue is taking place, who is present in each shot and what their character will be doing.

7 Once the scripts are ready, ask each group to read their work aloud. Encourage the rest of the class to listen out for any errors and provide feedback.

8 Depending on the number of learners and the equipment available, tell the learners either that, in the following class they will be filming their adverts and that they will need to bring any props, clothing or special items they require, or that they will film their adverts outside of class time and bring them to the following lesson. If the filming is to be done in class, a green screen should be used so that learners can place an image of a 1950s setting behind them to add authenticity.

9 Ask each group to upload and share their adverts on the class channel.

9.4 Off-duty avatars

Outline	Learners interview each other in the role of video-game characters, with green screen images of the game environment behind them to illustrate what they talk about. The premise is that their character has just finished a hard day at work and is being interviewed about it.
Primary focus	Asking and answering questions; narrating a first-person story; describing daily routine; verb tenses; construction of questions
Secondary focus	Language related to video-game play
Time	2 × 60 minutes
Level	Intermediate and above
Preparation	You will need a green screen, images of scenes from video games, a smartphone or other portable device with video-recording capability and also laptops or tablets for the editing stage. Learners should try to mimic the appearance of their chosen video game characters.

Procedure

1 Ask learners to think of a video game they enjoy playing. Select individuals to describe their chosen game and explain what they like about it.

2 Ask learners to choose a video-game character they know well and think about the actions he or she can perform and to write these down. Common examples may include: climb walls, run, jump, collect things, shoot, drive vehicles. Provide a short time limit (about 10 minutes) for this step.

3 Ask the learners the following questions: *If you could interview a video-game character, what character would it be? What would you ask?*

4 Tell learners to work with a partner (who has chosen a different character) to create questions to ask each other in an interview. These interviews will take place at the end of a 'day's work' for the character and will focus on what he or she has done that day. Provide help with the language and construction of the questions where needed and then allow time (about 20 minutes) for learners to rehearse their interviews.

5 Explain that in the next class the interviews will be performed and filmed. Ask learners to bring any props or clothing they have that might be associated with their character.

6 In the next class, film the characters being interviewed in front of the green screen. The interviewer can remain off camera if they prefer, as they will change roles after they have interviewed their partner.

7 Send learners their green screen video files (use a file-sharing service such as file2send.eu or wetransfer.com to do this as they will be too large to email) so that they can edit in background scenes from the video games that illustrate what they say in the interviews.

8 Ask each group to upload and share their interviews on the class channel.

Variation 1

For lower-level learners, the interviews could be about a typical daily routine for their chosen character, using present tenses instead of past tenses.

Variation 2

If your learners have never played a video game, they could, instead, play the roles of movie stars from specific genres (action, western, horror, etc.). In Step 2, the learners would then brainstorm typical actions performed by characters in these types of film.

9.5 The egg challenge

Outline	Learners design, engineer and present a solution to the problem of protecting an egg from breaking when dropped from the height of a first-floor window.
Primary focus	Language for collaborating on a task, giving opinions, asking for the opinions of others, agreeing, disagreeing, justifying and clarifying viewpoints; presenting to an audience; describing a process; practising conditional clauses
Secondary focus	Creative, divergent thinking; design skills; anticipating problems and proposing potential solutions; testing hypotheses. This project is also ideal for preparing learners for Parts 2 and 3 of the Cambridge First (FCE) speaking test.
Time	Approx 3 × 60 minutes
Level	Intermediate and above
Preparation	You will need three pieces of A4 paper, a roll of sticky tape, a pair of scissors and an egg for each group, as well as one empty cardboard egg box. Felt pens can also be used to personalize the shells of the eggs if the learners wish. One smartphone or video camera is needed for filming. A large piece of plastic can be used both as a target and also to make it easy to clean up the less successful design solutions. For an example video of my learners completing the egg challenge, see: youtu.be/bp4fmy9ISss

Procedure

1 Show learners the cardboard egg box and ask them if they think it is a good design (it is – you don't often find broken eggs inside them). Ask why they think it might have been designed that way. Encourage them to think about the following points and elicit feedback:

the choice of material
how the shape helps to keep the eggs separate
how the top and bottom halves are designed to meet to form a protective casing
what forces and impacts the boxes were designed to resist

Provide language 'just in time' as the speakers attempt to express their thoughts. The key point here is that everything about the object was a deliberate and rational design choice.

2 Ask learners if they think an egg placed inside the box would survive being dropped from a first-floor window (highly unlikely).

3 Tell learners that they are going to attempt to design a superior protective casing for the egg that will survive a drop from this distance and possibly higher. The catch is that they are only allowed to use the following equipment:

Three pieces of A4 paper
One small roll of sticky tape
Scissors (for cutting the paper, they cannot be part of the design solution)

They must also follow the rule that the sticky tape cannot be in contact with the egg. As learners will be using paper as their primary design material, pre-teach the following vocabulary or elicit it through demonstration:

> *tear (in half / into strips / up / a hole in)*
> *rip (in half / into pieces)*
> *fold (in half / into quarters / into a fan shape)*
> *crumple (up)*
> *cut (into pieces / off the corners / down the middle / along the edge)*
> *roll (up / into tubes)*

4   Give learners 15 minutes to brainstorm ideas with their partners. They must either agree on one design to present to the rest of the class or agree to disagree and present both solutions. Monitor and assist with language as necessary. When the time is up, allow them to use the board to sketch their ideas and explain their prototype designs and the decisions and assumptions they are based on. Encourage the rest of the class to try to identify potential problems with their solution.

5   At the end of the class, tell learners to think about the solutions presented by their colleagues and to reflect on how they might improve their own designs in preparation to build them in the next lesson. Encourage the pairs of learners to communicate and collaborate using social media tools (Google Docs is ideal for this).

6   At the beginning of the next class, distribute the three pieces of A4 paper, small roll of sticky tape and pair of scissors to each pair of learners. Provide them with a time limit (30–40 minutes is usually sufficient) to build their designs. Instead of monitoring, at this stage move around the room, filming and interviewing the learners about what they are doing. To avoid unanticipated breakages, provide learners with the eggs only at the point when they need to close or seal their designs.

7   When the time limit has expired, each group presents their final design solution, explaining their thought processes and any ideas they may have rejected or found unworkable along the way. Film these presentations to provide a record of the learners' language and presentation skills and also to share on the class channel.

8   Take learners to the 'drop zone' and lay out the plastic target on the floor. Film learners dropping their eggs one at a time (inside their protective packaging) and their reactions when they see the results of their efforts. Finally, when all the learners' eggs have been dropped, a volunteer drops the last egg inside the original egg box.

Follow-up
Interview learners about what worked well (or didn't) and how they might do things differently if they were given another opportunity.

Note
Don't be afraid to use this project with adult groups. In my experience they have thoroughly enjoyed it and produced at least as much language as younger learners!

9.6 Invader

Outline	This is a street game in which learners record reconnaissance videos in the role of aliens planning to invade Earth. These videos are narrated as they are recorded, and learners make their observations as though they are seeing and interpreting the human world for the first time. An example of a video made by one of my adult learners can be viewed here: youtu.be/woWoTDBMakE
Primary focus	The game is an end in itself, in that it provides a fun, engaging opportunity for embodied, situated language emergence. It also reinforces the notion that English is not just something to be studied abstractly in the classroom. The game can, however, also be integrated into the curriculum to focus on specific language structures.
Secondary focus	Raising awareness of habitual errors (by using the recorded material for subsequent language analysis in class)
Time	60 minutes (preparation) + 90 minutes (game)
Level	Intermediate and above
Preparation	This game works best when played in a busy, urban location such as a town centre, raising possible safety and permission issues for younger learners. Make sure that proper parental consent is gained and learners stay in groups. Alternatively, *Invader* can be played within the school building and grounds or a shopping centre if bad weather is expected. Smartphones with video-recording capability will be needed, which can be shared if necessary.
	Setting up the game: Design cards containing a map of the area you would like learners to investigate. Include tick boxes for them to record their progress. Some examples can be downloaded at: bit.ly/invadercards. I chose to demarcate the invasion zone in the shape of a space invader just for fun. Sign in to Google Maps, click on the 'Create map' button and use the drawing tool to outline whatever shape you like. You can also mark points of interest by dropping markers on the map and add GPS coordinates to the cards to guide learners there. Print the cards on sturdy paper, preferably in colour.

Procedure

1 Learners play the role of an alien race that has infiltrated the local human population in order to collect reconnaissance data to prepare for an imminent full-scale invasion. In the lesson preceding the game, outline this scenario and ask learners to brainstorm and discuss details regarding the origins and name of their species and the reason why they intend to invade planet Earth.

2 Project or display three images, one of a human performing an action (such as sweeping the floor or speaking on the phone), one of a human artefact (such as a dustbin or postbox) and one of a human space (a square or a park for example). See page 188 for some examples.

3 Ask learners to imagine that they have never witnessed these strange things before and give them five minutes to think of possible interpretations that an alien might have of them. These should include not only what they can see, but also conjecture regarding the possible purpose or function of the human action, artefact or space being documented and how this might impact on their plans for invasion. When the time is up, ask them to share their ideas with the class. They should do this in character, always referring to people as 'the humans' or 'aliens'.

Language Learning with Digital Video

Figure 9.1: Example images for *Invader*

4 Agree on a convenient place and time to meet on the day of the game and tell learners what equipment to bring. Also, make sure they know how to use their devices to record video and remind them to check that they are fully charged.

5 When everyone has arrived, give each learner an invader card (see 'Preparation' on page 187 and an example on page 189) and establish a time limit. Around 45 minutes to an hour should be sufficient. Arrange a place to meet at the end of the mission or agree to meet back in the classroom if this is practical. Ask your learners to run a quick equipment check to make sure that everything is working. If any equipment is malfunctioning the learners can agree to share devices.

6 Send learners off to complete their mission. During the game the role of the teacher becomes that of a participant observer, filming and photographing events and assisting with language and equipment when necessary.

7 When all the learners have arrived at the meeting point, return to the classroom. If necessary, early finishers can include an extra description of a human, an action, an artefact or a space around the meeting point while they wait.

8 Learners import their media into their video-editing software and add titles to complete their invader reconnaissance reports. These can then be uploaded to the class channel and embedded on a webpage dedicated to the project. If no more time is available this stage can also be completed in the following class.

Follow-up
Learners can explore each other's reports and suggest alternative interpretations of the actions, artefacts and spaces described.

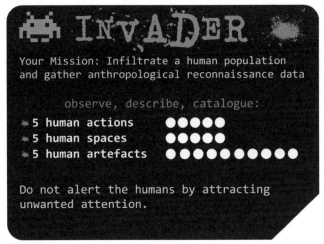

Front

Figure 9.2: Example of an Invader card

Variation

As a more ambitious variation of this, I often create a collaborative Google Map and ask my learners to embed their media and place it at the precise location in which it was produced. This serves as a form of memory archive of the route they took and can also be annotated. The same map can be used for multiple games to build up a more detailed view of human culture and behaviour over time. You can easily embed text, geo-tagged Flickr photo sets, YouTube clips and audio recordings on a shared map. An example of a collaborative Invader map can be viewed here: youtu.be/6Dg-29a92GM

9.7 Half-baked remake

Outline	Learners create quick and inexpensive two-minute remakes of famous Hollywood movies.
Primary focus	Narrative devices (verb tenses, connectors, etc.); dialogue writing/performing
Secondary focus	Making a summary; retelling a story
Time	Approximately 90 minutes
Level	Elementary and above
Preparation	You will need a video camera, smartphone or tablet with sound- and video-recording capability.

Procedure

1 Show learners this YouTube clip of someone, who hasn't seen any of the *Star Wars* films, explaining the story of the original trilogy: youtu.be/FJTCYdZTj2A (For a slightly more up-to-date film, this video of someone's mother trying to explain the plot of *The Matrix* is also fun: youtu.be/OMf9GlLXouA.) Elicit feedback as to the accuracy of the narrator's version of the actual plot of the films. Those who have seen the films are likely to think these clips are funny and confused attempts, while those who have not are likely to think they sound about right.

2 Ask learners to form groups of three or four. Set a five-minute time limit and tell each learner to explain the story of a well-known film that they have only heard of, but that at least one other member of their group has already seen. Learners take it in turns to be the narrator or the listener. Explain that accuracy is not important and that they should just make up any details that they don't know.

3 Tell learners that they are now going to plan and film a two-minute remake of a famous Hollywood film. As an example show the trailer of the 2008 film *Be Kind Rewind* (youtu.be/J7C8nHAAs70), which tells the story of two video-rental shop workers who accidentally erase all of the video cassettes. To avoid being fired they re-shoot every film in the shop with their own camera on a budget of nothing.

4 Check to see how many film remakes they spotted in the clip: *Ghostbusters*, *Robocop*, *Rush Hour 2*, *2001 A Space Odyssey*, *Boyz N The Hood*, *Driving Miss Daisy*, *Silence of The Lambs*.

5 In their groups, learners agree on a famous film they would like to remake. It doesn't matter if multiple groups select the same film, as each version is likely to be idiosyncratic enough to distinguish it from the others. Once they have selected a film, tell them to write a short summary (40–60 words) of the film plot. Refer them to the imdb.com site if they need inspiration, as each page begins with a short plot summary. Here's an example summary:

> **The Hunger Games**
>
> Every year in the nation of Panem twelve boys and twelve girls are randomly selected to take part in the televised 'Hunger Games'. When Katniss Everdeen's sister is chosen, Katniss knows she has to take her sister's place in order to protect her from the brutal televised fight for survival.

6   Explain that each member of the group will have a speaking part (possibly more than one if more characters are needed than group members) and that the dialogue should be improvised rather than copied from the original script. They will also have to find appropriate locations and improvised props to shoot their remake. The more basic, cheap and amateurish the film looks, the better the end result will be.

7   Using their previously written short summaries as storyboards, learners make their own version of the film they selected (outside of class time), edit it (adding any music, special effects or titles) and upload it to the class channel.

8   Set up a webpage or blog dedicated to this project and embed the learners' videos. Include a poll so that learners can vote for the best (or worst!) acting, special effects, soundtrack, script and film.

9   In the next class, screen the remakes and announce the winners.

9.8 Coming up...

Outline	Learners choose a theme they are interested in and then plan and create a video podcast. This can be either a one-off activity or a weekly/monthly show that runs throughout the course.
Primary focus	Specific language related to show hosting (current affairs, music, cinema, technology, etc.)
Secondary focus	Using expressive body language, gesture and intonation
Time	2 × 60 minutes
Level	Elementary and above
Preparation	You will need to find two or three example clips of good video podcasts, making sure that the content is suitable for your learners' age group. Try to choose examples in which the presenter or presenters are visible, as opposed to just providing a voice-over. Also choose ones that have a clear structure. Here are a few examples: Geekbeat: geekbeat.tv/wireless-sensor-for-your-dog Tech News Today: twit.tv/show/tech-news-today/833 Fact or Fictional: revision3.com/factorfictional/spider-man

Procedure

1 Write the term 'video podcast' on the board or screen and ask learners if they are familiar with the term or can guess its meaning.

2 Show learners your example podcast clips and ask them to answer the following questions as they watch. Run through them first to check for comprehension:

Does the show have ...
   ... an intro theme tune?
   ... a welcome message?
   ... announcements about past content?
   ... announcements about the topics to be covered in the current episode?
   ... co-hosts?
   ... sponsors?

3 Explain that these are typical examples of the structure of the beginning of a video podcast show. They are often followed by:

Middle:
The latest news relating to the topic
Tips on how to do something related to the topic (e.g. the best ways to buy concert tickets online in a music-themed show)
An interview
A review

End:
Final comments and teaser for the next episode
Theme music

4   Tell learners that they are going to plan and create their own three- to five-minute video podcasts. Ask them to form pairs or groups of three and to brainstorm ideas for the theme of their show. This should be a topic that they are enthusiastic about and something that they think other people will also find interesting or useful. Monitor and help out with language and ideas. For those struggling to come up with something, popular broad themes are:

Cinema   *Music*   *Video games*   *Technology*   *Apps*   *Sports*

Once they have agreed on a topic, ask them to choose a name for their show that in some way will reflect its content. For more advanced learners, challenge them to use alliteration or rhyme in their titles, as seen in the three example podcasts in 'Preparation' on page 192: Geekbeat (rhyme), Tech News Today (alliteration), Fact or Fictional (alliteration).

5   In their pairs or groups, learners plan the segments and provisional ideas for the content of their show. Direct them once more to the *beginning*, *middle* and *end* structure outlined on page 192. They do not have to stick to this rigidly, but it can serve as a guide and help them break the planning of their show into smaller and more manageable chunks.

6   Once learners have produced a rough outline of their show, they can begin scripting their parts. Refer them to the example podcasts and tell them to listen and note down any language they think might be useful. Examples of set phrases from Tech News Today include:

Coming up on Tech News today…
All that and more, coming up.
This is Tech News Today for Thursday July 5th…
Welcome to Tech News Today. I'm…
Starting with the top ten stories of the day…
Joining us now to discuss the stories of the day we have…
Let's finish up by talking about…

While planning their scripts, learners will need to consider how to divide their roles. If they are working in pairs, it is usually helpful for one to be responsible for framing and filming the shots while the other presents a segment before swapping roles. Groups of three may want to have two learners co-hosting on screen while the third member takes charge of the camera before being interviewed or presenting a specialist segment.

7   Allow time for learners to rehearse their scripts. Refer them once more to the example video podcasts, but this time instruct them to pay close attention to the gestures, body posture, facial expressions and vocal intonation of the show hosts. For example, how does the host of Tech News Today say, '*All that and more, coming up.*'? What does Cali Lewis do with her hands when she says, '*Welcome to Geekbeat!*'? People who are inexperienced in speaking to a camera often tense up and I have found that attempting to impersonate the gestures and facial expressions of relaxed and natural presenters can build confidence, improve oral fluency and help them to use more natural intonation in their speech. Move between groups and provide language support and advice as needed.

8 With smaller classes the video podcasts can be filmed in the classroom in front of a green screen so that learners can substitute the background with images or video clips that illustrate the content of their show. If this is not practical, learners can arrange to film their shows at home, either together or separately in segments. If filmed at home, a television or computer monitor can be used to display a green background (as in Geekbeat), allowing the learners to treat it as they would a green screen.

9 In the following class, learners bring their raw footage and work on editing the show together. Although this could easily be achieved outside of class, I have found this to be a key phase of language production. Dozens of decisions need to be negotiated and agreed upon when editing together even short video podcasts. Theme music will need to be selected, segments will need to be reordered and shortened, titles and 'lower thirds' (superimposed text at the bottom of the screen) added and media chosen to replace the green screen backgrounds.

10 Learners upload and share their video podcasts to the class channel.

Figure 9.3: Podcast produced by learner

Note
Video podcasts are (usually) short video shows distributed online, often in the form of daily or weekly episodes. While they were originally quite amateurish, now with even the most basic video-editing software and equipment, individuals can produce quality content and reach a global audience for almost any niche topic imaginable, from robotics to origami.

Sources

Viewing and sharing

There are alternatives to YouTube! For viewing and sharing videos, you could also look at the following:

Vimeo (vimeo.com)
The emphasis here is on quality over quantity. It has a more professional interface than YouTube with a very good range of short films from new directors, experimental videos and interesting new genres. With regard to searching for videos, a good place to start is with the 'Staff Picks' section (vimeo.com/channels/staffpicks). The great thing about Vimeo is the player itself: unlike on YouTube, for example, there are very few adverts which can distract you, so the viewing is much more pleasurable and user-friendly.

Dailymotion (dailymotion.com)
This site offers videos of varying length organized by category. There is a good mix of professionally made and amateur clips.

WatchKnowLearn (watchknowlearn.org)
This site provides free educational videos for kids (both primary and secondary).

Flickr (flickr.com/explore/video)
Better known as a photo-sharing site, this site also has space for you to watch and upload videos.

Storycorps (storycorps.org)
This site allows people of all kinds to share their stories online. Although mainly audio, there are also animated videos based around true life histories: storycorps.org/animation.

Lesson plans and clips for language learning

Film English (film-english.com)
Kieran Donaghy's site contains ready-made lesson plans based around short films.

Lessonstream (lessonstream.org)
Jamie Keddie's site includes a lot of work with video.

allatc (allatc.wordpress.com)
Steve Muir and Tom Spain's Activities for Advanced Learners also include a lot of work with video.

Elteachertrainer (elteachertrainer.com)
John Hughes's blog includes a lot of great ideas for working with video.

Movie Segments to Assess Grammar Goals (moviesegmentstoassessgrammargoals.blogspot.com.br)
Claudio Azevedo's site looks at how short movie clips contextualize different grammar structures.

Simple English Videos (simpleenglishvideos.com)
This site includes clickable transcripts and a great selection of movie trailers and music videos, as well as specially made films which focus on particular language points or structures.

Vicki Hollett (vickihollett.com)
Vicki Hollett's site has a range of downloadable materials for Business English teaching.

EFL Classroom (community.eflclassroom.com/video)
This site has an enormous range of video clips to check out and includes an ad-free YouTube player with some interesting clips at: eflclassroom.com/youtube

Commercial sites

English Central (englishcentral.com)
This site boasts thousands of video lessons and video courses. There is a whole host of material available, though some of it is intended for learner self-study including intensive work on speaking and pronunciation.

English Attack (english-attack.com)
This site includes a range of video lessons but with an emphasis on gaming and social media.

Learner-created videos

Next Vista for Learning (nextvista.org)
This is a great site which organizes video-making contests and includes videos divided into three categories: 1   Light Bulbs: for videos that teach you how to do something.
2   Global Views: videos created to promote understanding of cultures.
3   Seeing Service: highlights the work of people who are making a difference in the lives of others.

GoAnimate (goanimate.com)
Artoonix (artoonix.com)
Zimmer Twins (zimmertwins.com/movie/create)
These three sites allow learners to create their own animated stories.

Content

General educational
Archive (archive.org/details/movies)
A digital archive with downloadable content, including film, documentaries, animation and sports.

Big Think (bigthink.com)
For ideas, interviews, presentations and video features.

National Archives (nationalarchives.gov.uk)
A comprehensive UK video archive.

British Pathé Film Archive (youtube.com/britishpathe
85,000 films now freely available online via a YouTube channel.

Activism
It Gets Better Project (itgetsbetter.org)
Campaign for equality and visibility.

Take Part (takepart.com)
Includes many videos on different campaigns.

Uncultured Project (youtube.com/user/UnculturedProject)

Art
The Creator's Project (thecreatorsproject.vice.com/video)

Google Art Project (google.com/culturalinstitute/project/art-project)

Cinema and television
Netflix (netflix.com)
Streamed TV shows and movies, available in the US, Latin America and parts of Europe.

Hulu (hulu.com)
Streamed TV and video content in the US and Japan.

BBC (bbc.co.uk/iplayer/tv) (only UK)

Public Broadcasting Service (video.pbs.org) (only US)

BlipTV (blip.tv)
Video content series covering animation, comedy, drama, entertainment, food, music, etc.

Vice (vice.com/en_uk/video)
Popular alternative clips and TV shows.

How-to
Videojug (videojug.com)

Howcast (howcast.com)

My Best Idea (ivillage.com/my-best-idea)

Ideas
Idea channel (youtube.com/user/pbsideachannel)

Good (good.is/video)

Wired (video.wired.com)

Google (youtube.com/user/Google)
Includes stories from Google Maps developers.

Kids

NatGeo (kids.nationalgeographic.com/kids)

PBS kids (pbskids.org/video) (only in the US)

Teen (teen.com/videos)

Sesame Street (sesamestreet.org/videos)

Music

Vevo (vevo.com)
Currently the best site to watch music videos.

Pitchfork (pitchfork.com/tv)
A range of music videos, documentaries and interviews.

Nature

Life on Terra (lifeonterra.com)
Wonderful vignettes of the people, places and animals that make up the heart and soul of life on earth.

Explore (explore.org)
High-quality documentary films focusing on the work of non-profit organizations around the world.

National Geographic (video.nationalgeographic.com)

BBC Nature (bbc.co.uk/nature/collections/p0085nk0)
BBC site which includes time-lapse photography.

News

Video content from news media groups such as:

The Guardian (theguardian.com/video)

The New York Times (nytimes.com/video)

Reuters (reuters.com/news/video/reuters-tv)

For alternatives try:
Newsy (newsy.com)

Live leak (liveleak.com)

Huffington Post (live.huffingtonpost.com)

Science

Periodic Videos (periodicvideos.com)
A periodic table of entertaining videos from the University of Nottingham (also on YouTube: youtube.com/user/periodicvideos).

NASA (climate.nasa.gov/climate_reel)
A range of videos on global climate change.

Scientific American (scientificamerican.com/multimedia)

Wired (wired.com/category/wiredscience)

Short films
FILMS short (filmsshort.com)
Short of the Week (shortoftheweek.com)
The Smalls (thesmalls.com)
These three sites allow you to search for short films via category and genre.

Speeches and talks
American Rhetoric (americanrhetoric.com)
A wonderful resource full of speeches from all genres.

TED Talks (ted.com/talks)
TED Ed (ed.ted.com)
For TED talks and lessons based around TED videos.

Five-minute Debates (theguardian.com/commentisfree/series/five-minute-debates)
A range of formal five-minute debates and face-to-face discussions with experts in particular fields.

TrueTube (truetube.co.uk)
For less formal discussions on many topics taught in schools, including citizenship, religion and PSHE (Personal, Social and Health Education).

Sport
ESPN (espn.go.com/30for30)
Award-winning short film collection based on sports and sporting heroes.

Footytube (footytube.com)
Not just the goals!

Travel
The Vagabond Project (thevagabondproject.tv)
Web-based collective showing insights into world travel for young people.

The Dime Traveler (thedimetraveler.com)
Good for teenagers.

David's Been Here (youtube.com/user/Davidsbeenhere)
A genuinely informative travel blog.

Finally, please go to the book's companion website (digitalv.net) for more ideas and inspiration for sourcing and using video in your classes.

Index

Note: Activity titles are shown in **bold**.